M000208990

WILL

I BE THE

HERO

OF MY OWN

LIFE?

WILL
I BE THE
HERO
OF MY OWN
LIFE?

Swami Chetananānda

Edited by Linda L. Barnes

RUDRA PRESS
PORTLAND, OREGON

Rudra Press
P.O. Box 13390
Portland, OR 97213
Telephone: (503) 235-0175
Telefax: (503) 235-0909

The following publishers have generously given permission to use quotations from
copyrighted works:

From *Bhagavad Gita* as translated by Winthrop Sargeant. By permission of the
State University of New York Press. Copyright © 1984.

From *Sanskrit Poetry from Vidyakra's "Treasury"* translated by Daniel Ingalls,
Cambridge, MA. Reprinted by permission of the Belknap Press of Harvard
University Press. Copyright © 1965, 1968 by the President and Fellows of
Harvard College.

Editor: Linda L. Barnes
Cover Design: Milton Glaser
Book Design: Bill Stanton

Library of Congress Cataloging-in-Publication Data
Chetanananda, Swami, 1948-
    Will I be the hero of my own life? / Swami Chetanananda :
edited by Linda L. Barnes
    p.   cm.
    Includes bibliographical references.
    ISBN 0-915801-38-8
    1. Spiritual life. 2. Heroism—Religious aspects. I. Barnes,
Linda L.   II. Title.
BL624.C454 1995   95-23272
294.5'44—dc20   CIP

00 99 98   10 9 8 7 6 5 4 3 2

CONTENTS

Each piece of work that our lives brings us is a chance to be buried or a chance to be free...I would add to this that spiritual work is a work that should not be left undone. —*Swami Chetanananda*

WILL I BE THE HERO of my own life? A very profound question. Swami Chetanananda is both asking us and challenging us to pause and reflect on the very purpose of our existence. Am I able to say that I am really taking advantage of the gift of life I was given? Will I be my own life's hero? Will I be brave enough to overcome all obstacles and attain the highest benefit from this life's experience?

What we want to find is what Buddha referred to as the middle way: to be in the stillness of the center.

If I was training to win an Olympic gold medal, I would read about the history of my event and study the form and practices of previous winners. I would make a deep commitment to persevere and sustain the necessary effort to attain my goal. I would find the world's best instructor to teach and guide me in those precise techniques that worked for others. To reach my goal, I would be prepared to make the enormous sacrifices that would take me through the difficult process of growing and changing my physical and mental conditions. I know that muscles would have to be stretched correctly, that I would have to learn to breathe differently, that I would have to learn to control my mind and adopt a totally new mental attitude about myself and my life. I understand that I would have to apply myself diligently to the rigors of training and practice every single day for years and years.

Winning a gold medal would surely be wonderful. But would it make me the hero of my own life? Would it sustain me through the pain and suffering that accompany us through life?

> In the deepest sense, the same crystallized energy that represents tension, stress, pain, and suffering—when released—has the potential to uplift us and expand our awareness…The way we change is by releasing the tensions within ourselves as we go through our day. We relax and open our hearts to everything.

Swami Chetanananda asks us to be as determined about growing spiritually as we are about succeeding in our physical and material lives. He talks carefully, from his own experience, about how to direct our attention inward and discover a personal path to our own divinity. In my mind, this is what it really means to be a hero to ourselves. It really means discovering our divinity. It means discovering and pursuing our own unlimited inner potential as it unfolds for each of us. It means becoming the best person we can be.

> When we open ourselves through our spiritual practice, we start to bring our attention inside and keep it there. Slowly, with our breathing and concentration, we release the tensions within us, opening deeper channels of creative energy, creative awareness, and creative expression. Slowly, our intellectual, emotional, and operational boundaries start to dissolve.

Throughout *Will I Be the Hero of My Own Life?*, the author refers to Arjuna, hero of the Bhagavad Gita, struggling to understand his own purpose in life. In the guise of Arjuna's chariot driver, Lord Krishna represents a higher spiritual understanding. Just as Krishna for Arjuna clears away the mist from the mysteries of life, Swami Chetanananda guides us toward recognizing what we must do to realize our own potential. He clarifies life's purpose in a very real and practical way.

> Wherever I sit in meditation becomes the sacrificial fire pit. The sacrificial wood is my breath. The sacrifice is my

own awareness of myself, which I burn up with conscious effort and concentration. This rises into the heavenly sphere and provokes a response from the Divine in the outpouring of creative energy.

Winning a gold medal can certainly be a mission in life. However, my goal is to be at peace with myself and with others, to be happy and to do good work, to achieve the highest state of awareness possible for me, and to continually reach for a higher state of spiritual fulfillment.

> Having a spiritual life is simply integrating our ordinary lives more and more deeply into the flow of our own creative energy as it unfolds its highest potential.

This book exhilarates me. It is an invitation to breathe deeply from life's experiences, to live more fully and to live well. It offers a way to help us find our own inner resource. The words are clear and simple, direct and personal. To read them is to have a stimulating and satisfying heart-to-heart talk with someone who wishes us well, with someone who lives an exemplary life and knows from whence he is talking.

> There is but one soul, and everything around us is an articulation of its pure creative power. To find within ourselves that one soul is to find the same power and joy that created the whole universe. In that state, there is nothing lacking, nothing to add, nothing that can ever be taken away.

Once in a rare while, a person devotes his or her life not only to attaining a personal state of freedom and release but also to helping others attain that same state. Without being wrapped in a dogma or any philosophical restrictions, Swami Chetanananda has literally reached out into the cosmos to attain for himself and others that energy that opens us all to our highest state of awareness. I met Swamiji in 1971 when I was a student of Swami Rudrananda (Rudi). Rudi died in 1973 and since then I have had the privilege of knowing, traveling with, and studying with Swamiji. I am continually amazed at his ability to articulate and reduce the seemingly complex life we all share to one of simplicity, beauty, and love.

I do hope you will enjoy this wonderful book and find guidance to help make your journey here successful.

Norman Bodek
President
Productivity, Inc.

URING THE SUMMER of 1992, hundreds of Swami Chetanananda's students gathered at his retreat center on Martha's Vineyard to honor Chetanananda's own teacher, Swami Rudrananda (Rudi). In a beautiful clearing in the woods overlooking Menemsha Bay, a newly built shrine honoring Rudi was blessed; the shrine further established Rudi's presence as a felt and living reality.

During the following weeks, Chetanananda led a series of seminars, introducing his students to new themes and reformulations of earlier teachings. The imagery he used was startling, even shocking, while at the same time deeply provocative. He spoke eloquently of early spiritual seekers and practitioners in India who came out of warrior training and later pursued their practice in a radically different way by going into the cremation grounds and confronting their own attachments and limitations in the face of death. At the root of their search was the question of what it meant to live as the hero of your own life. Arjuna, the warrior protagonist of the Bhagavad Gita, faced the same question in his epic story.

Our relationship to our own actions, our sense of attachment to their outcomes, our capacity for openness to much deeper processes, are the issues here. The true hero is one whose life is oriented by a commitment to the highest best interest of the whole, one who serves the greater process of Life Itself. This commitment brings about a thorough re-examination of our role in relation to others and of the real value of what we hold onto, whether our attachments be to people, positions, or various forms of power. As Chetanananda points out, we need not abandon any of these elements of our lives; but without a true understanding of their limitations and of our own, we remain bound in ways that constrain the very real possibilities of freedom available to all concerned.

Chetanananda's discussions that summer of 1992 provided the initial impetus for this book; the following summer, he delved more deeply into the theme of the quality of life that emerges when we learn to free ourselves from our efforts to manipulate and control outcomes. Why is this important? Because the very effort to control events means that we restrict ourselves and others to the current level of our own imagination. We fail to recognize other possibilities inherent in a situation because we are too busy trying to make it turn out the way we think we want it to. We stifle the deeper creative potential that Life Itself embeds in every event. We miss those moments of grace when true inspiration might flash forth, illuminating unforeseen and unimagined outcomes that are, in fact, altogether possible.

As Chetanananda suggests, to be the hero of our own lives is to free ourselves to be alive to such inspiration. It is to open our hearts to the presence of grace and to respond to that presence wholeheartedly. Doing so takes us back into the heart of what it means to serve the whole, a whole that includes ourselves. It means being willing to live with uncertainty because there is no freedom without uncertainty. But in that freedom, we open ourselves to pass from the battlefield of the warrior, into the cremation ground and, from there, to live as the hero of a truly inspired life.

Linda L. Barnes
Editor

THE HERO

of your own

LIFE

IN MANY OF the ancient myths of India, Greece, Rome, and other cultures, there are often central characters called heroes, many of whom were also warriors. Heroes are people who, in a real way, have confronted and changed their identities through the process of some kind of intense difficulty that they have had to undergo. This intense difficulty is sometimes consciously chosen and accepted; at other times, it is just thrust upon a person. But it is a difficulty that such people endure because they have certain ideals to which they cling and which they refuse to give up, no matter what. However impossible the endeavor, they take on the challenge and digest whatever hardships they are called upon to endure. In the process, they find within themselves a sense of strength that allows them to shed who and what they were, thereby becoming a completely different kind of person—a hero.

One of the great heroes of all literature appears in the Bhagavad Gita, a part of the ancient Indian epic the Mahabharata, which tells the story of the warrior Arjuna. The story begins as Arjuna finds himself out on the battlefield in the midst of a war between two branches of his extended family. As he sits in his chariot accompanied by his charioteer—who is actually the god Krishna, he looks out upon the carnage that the members of his clan are wreaking upon each other and realizes that he cannot find a way to justify entering the fight. How, he asks, can he kill his cousins, his uncles? A highly trained warrior, he nevertheless sits down in his chariot to brood upon this question.

> Having seen this, my own people, Krishna,
> Desiring to fight, approaching,
> My limbs sink down
> And my mouth dries up
> And my body trembles
> And my hair stands on end...
> I do not desire to kill

Them who are bent on killing,
Slayer of Madhu (Krishna)…
Thus having spoken, in the battle,
Arjuna sat down upon the seat of the chariot,
Throwing down both arrow and bow,
With a heart overcome by sorrow.[1]

It is significant that the battlefield analogy is used in the Bhagavad Gita because here is Arjuna confronting his attachments, his own cognitive structures, his desires, his illusions, and his emotional entanglements. This is especially so because the people whom he faces on this battlefield are his teachers and his relatives. Even today in India, a person's extended family—the cousins and uncles, for example—is experienced as being the same as one's father and brothers. It is common for brother and brother to share the same house, for their children to grow up together, and for them to work together in the same business. In some of the languages of the subcontinent, there is not even a real word for "cousins." The word is simply "brother."

This gives us a better sense of the flavor of Arjuna's dilemma. He is confronting all that he loves and that with which he is totally identified. His family, his past, and his future are all there in front of him. These people have already done great damage to each other, and Arjuna sinks down in

---

[1] Winthrop Sargeant, trans., *Bhagavad Gita* (Albany: State University of New York Press, 1984), pp. 66-7, 85.

the middle of it, saying, "I can't do it. I can't go on with this any more." As Arjuna's charioteer Krishna is there to point out to him, however, he has no choice but to go on. He has been trained as a warrior and that is his role in this lifetime. The choice he faces is one of whether to play out that role well or badly, but play it he must. Krishna says:

> Better one's own duty deficient
> Than the duty of another caste well performed.
> Better death in one's own duty;
> The duty of another caste invites danger.[2]

At the same time, however, Arjuna can choose to conduct himself as a warrior in battle from a different state of awareness—a state that transcends the conflicts and the dilemma that he faces. If he can do this, then he will bring benefit not only to himself but also to his family and to those who love and are devoted to him. In doing this, he will be serving God.

Krishna takes a fairly gentle approach, patiently urging Arjuna to pick himself up and get on with his life. When one strategy fails to get Arjuna's attention, Krishna goes at it from another direction. Here they are out on the battlefield, with two huge armies facing off in the midst of brutality that has been going on for some time. Indeed, the violence in the Mahabharata far exceeds anything that

---

[2] *Bhagavad Gita*, Sargeant, p. 192.

happens on television or in the action movies. The story describes all the gory details of how one warrior or another flies into a rage and rips somebody else apart for having annoyed him. Furthermore, it describes all too precisely how each of them does so.

Krishna goes on to point out that, ultimately, it is the Divine that determines everything. The real cause of how circumstances work out does not lie within the realm of human desire or even human will. He then goes into an elaborate discussion of knowledge and action, pointing out that as long as we are alive, we cannot avoid acting.

> Indeed, no one, even in the twinkling of an eye,
> Ever exists without performing action;
> Everyone is forced to perform action,
> even that action which is against his will...[3]

Therefore, the only thing we can do with respect to our actions is to surrender our own desires, letting go of our attachments to the fruits of those actions, and remaining open to the outcome, whether this be positive or negative.

Krishna adds that all knowledge is limited to some degree by whatever we identify with. Any knowledge only becomes wisdom when we function in a state of surrender. When that is the case, then the real fusion of knowledge and action can become loving. So the fusion of knowledge and

---

[3] *Bhagavad Gita*, Sargeant, p. 162.

action is loving self-sacrifice, the sacrifice in which we ourselves are personally transformed.

Krishna teaches Arjuna about selfless service as one level in the fusion of knowledge and action. The second thing he teaches him about is meditation and, through meditation, the nature of wisdom. This discussion culminates in the chapter in which Krishna reveals his cosmic form to Arjuna—a form that shows the merging of destruction and creativity, of the horrific and the sublime, of terror and bliss. In so doing, Krishna shows Arjuna the endless re-creative capacity of the fundamental ground of Life, in which unity, integrity, and fulfillment are always present, whatever the phase of the creative expression. In this vision, questions that we all ask—like "What's going to happen to me?"—never arise, because there is nothing that is not the Self. The point is to understand that what is put forth or withdrawn neither adds to nor detracts from the Self. Rather it is nothing but the creative expression of the Self as a whole.

It is with Krishna's help that Arjuna finally comes to understand his own place in the larger picture. Indeed, the Bhagavad Gita stresses the important role that the teacher plays in the process of coming to this understanding. At the same time, it demonstrates that the teacher is only another emanation of that same cosmic unity whose foundation lies within one's own consciousness. The setting of the story, the battlefield, is nothing but our own individual life experience. The field of our individual awareness is that same field of struggle.

The conflict is the conflict that all of us feel, in thoughts like "How will I survive?" and "What is my responsibility to others?" The Bhagavad Gita takes the line that what is best for oneself is also best for everybody else, but points out that this has nothing to do with fulfilling our narrower desires, wants, or needs. It goes on to elaborate simply and clearly that what is best for a person, ultimately, is self-surrender. In an individual, this manifests through the discipline required by one's spiritual practice; in the world, it then expresses itself as selfless service. Ultimately, the two come together in the fusion of knowledge and action and the recognition of one's infinite potential. But the key here is always surrender, which the text suggests through the interplay between the personal and the Infinite, the interpersonal and the Divine.

The Bhagavad Gita says, first and foremost, that we have to take care of ourselves. But this may not mean exactly what we think it does. Arjuna, the highly trained and skilled warrior, is instructed by his teacher in the context of the battlefield, an analogy for the struggle of life, to pull himself together and get to work.

This is what you have trained your whole life to do, Krishna says. It doesn't matter who has presented themselves out there in front of you. What matters is that you do your work.

Each person is always responsible for himself or herself in every single setting. And there is no setting in which we are not compelled to work, no matter how intimate or personal it may be. Indeed, for an Indian, there can be no more personal a setting than the relationship with a sibling or a cousin. Yet even then, the text requires us to work and be responsible for not getting sucked into our own romantic illusions or accepting any false assumption about the nature of a relationship. It tells us over and over again that we are responsible for ourselves in every situation.

To take care of ourselves in no way promotes a selfish orientation. We find Krishna saying to Arjuna: "You have to do your best at what you have trained to do. You must do this because it will serve the lives of the people that your life is intended to serve, including those people who present themselves to you as your enemies. Even the people you kill are people you are serving—who have been presented before you by God to meet their death in you."

In saying this, I am not promoting violence. I am suggesting, however, that even in such situations there is an underlying unity we rarely recognize.

The true hero is a person whose deepest interest lies in knowing the Infinite and in knowing God.

⌒

Heroes are people who seek and acquire power to address the question of human suffering not merely for their own benefit. Rather, they rise to a level where they are willing to sacrifice themselves to benefit the whole and to use the power they attain for the sake of others.

Heroes transcend themselves. The arena in which this happens does not much matter. More importantly, they are capable of recognizing their own fear, weakness, selfishness, and self-absorption. They are able to suspend and transcend all of that in order to serve the legitimate needs of other people—often at their own expense.

As we deepen our understanding of what it means to be the hero in our own lives, we will find that our own self-respect, as well as the respect of others, will grow based on our capacity to transcend our narrower interests in a particular moment—to discover what others really want and to give it to them. In doing this, we learn to release our egos. And this takes a lot of watching and listening. This is awareness of the hero.

DESIRE

and

DISCRIMINATION

WHEN I ASK PEOPLE to tell me about themselves, usually they say something like "Well, I come from this or that place, and I did this or that thing, and I'm going here or there. I want this or that," and so on and so forth. We all tend to do this. We define ourselves in terms of our wants and our history—which is usually the history of our wants.

However, to really know ourselves, we have to rise above the wanting. To be the hero of our own life—to have any respect for ourselves as human beings—requires that we go beyond being caught by our wants and desires. Otherwise we only know ourselves as a whole set of wants and needs. As we get older, those wants and needs dry up, leaving us with a restless, uncomfortable feeling that there should have been more to life.

It is funny how all the things we think of as making us distinct and interesting people are really an expression of our limitations. We think that they make us unique when actually they make us just like everybody else. This misunderstanding is a good example of how our conditioning inverts the way we think of ourselves and what we value about our lives. I would suggest instead that what is really important about us is a finer, deeper, and far more subtle vital force—what I call the energy of Life Itself. All that we are is the expression of that vital force, and to know it deeply is to the know the deepest Self that underlies every individual self.

In every way, we have complete choice over how we direct our energy. And we don't have a chance when we focus on tension and stress, when we operate from a sense of separation and isolation or from a state of pain, or when we are moved by desire, need, or ambition to end our sense of isolation, separation, and pain. We only end up creating more pain for ourselves. That is the paradox—and it is a vicious cycle. Even when we enter an event with the highest motives and best intentions, if our actions are motivated by pain and suffering, in the long term we can only come back around to more pain and suffering.

Most of us spend a lot of time feeding our desires. Instead of learning to be quiet inside and to observe what we feel from that place of inner stillness, we pour our energy into feeding the desire itself. Once we concentrate on addressing that particular desire, our view of real opportunities becomes limited. We fail to see that fulfillment lies only within ourselves.

For example, we get hungry. We think, "I have to get something to eat now!" The minute that thought comes up, we start foraging. Usually we limit ourselves to looking for what we already assume to be edible. We no longer experience the full range of things that are, in fact, edible. Instead, we get stuck running around after what is familiar.

The problem with desire is that it steals our energy and puts it into illusions that come from our own minds. We then spend it reaching for one thing, pulling away from another, extending ourselves, or getting contracted in the process. In every case, however, all we are doing is creating internal imbalances and all kinds of strain. First comes the imbalance, then the strain.

The strain causes us to feel every type of pain and to get locked into tensions, which build up into denser and thicker layers. This experience in turn makes us think that life is happening to us and not from us. Instead of experiencing ourselves as the heroes of our own lives, we come to see ourselves as the victims of our lives.

And when we think that life is happening to us, we throw control and responsibility for it somewhere else—somewhere beyond the stars or maybe in the hands of some deity who is impossible to please. This makes our ultimate fate a hell. At the very least, we perceive others as having all kinds of power over us—when, in fact, they don't. Existing in such a condition of imbalance and strain, we can't help but repeat what I call the mantra of ignorance—"What's going to happen to me?"

As long as we are asking "What's going to happen to me?" we have an agenda. It doesn't matter how benevolent our agenda may be. Any agenda is going to get in our way because it will disturb our ability to develop the kind of discrimination necessary to facilitate fulfilling whatever our role or work may be.

Only non-attachment allows us to develop a fine sense of discrimination. This discrimination leads to penetrating insights in which we are able to see the patterns that life manifests without having the details obscure our vision. We recognize the importance of the patterns underlying the details. By seeing clearly and residing in harmony with the patterns of Life Itself, we avoid becoming distressed.

⌁

There is no problem with acting on any of our desires. We have to understand, though, that we don't have unlimited time and energy. Wherever we expend our energy is the place we are spending our inner resource. So, we have to think carefully about the things we are doing and the desires we choose to pursue. Do they really promote our good and the good of the people we love—or are we just mucking around? Because we don't have infinite resources or infinite time, we must truly value both the resources and the time we do have.

How can we tell what we are really about in this regard? For the most part, what we do during our day demonstrates what we are attached to. I sometimes ask "What do you love?" as a way of getting people to think about their basic orientation. For that matter, in every moment the tensions that we experience ask us the same question: What do we love? If we really love God—if we really love Life—then each pulsation, each ripple in the vital force of our lives, is a source of excitement and exuberance, a condensation of joy. If we love something finite, however, then each pulsation and ripple in the force is liable to cause us some misery.

This is because these ripples and shifts will seem to threaten something in our lives. That something will seem to be moving in closer or going further away. Either may make us happy for a moment, but in the next moment we fall— because whatever comes closer also goes away. Likewise, whatever goes away and leaves us alone can always circle back in on us.

The energies that emerge from within and attach us to external things are like lines of force. Even as they emerge, they become something we will eventually have to surrender because only by surrendering them will we be able to grow. Whatever we think is important to us in life—whatever we think is important to do or to have—only obstructs our inner work until we release that sense of necessity. Note, by the way, that I did not say that we have to let go of the thing itself. As Krishna points out to Arjuna, the issue is our ability to act without attachment to the outcome of our actions.

Sometimes it is not a behavior that we are talking about giving up, but the attachment to that behavior. Of course that may require, at some stage, that we drop specific forms of behavior at specific points in time. We do so not as a general denial of that form of behavior, but as a test of our own attachment. So, although behavior itself is not the issue, we still may have to let go of something that is inappropriate to our overall development.

We can have our love affairs, we can pursue our careers, we can follow our hobbies and artistic interests—as long as we have a deeper inner base from which we actively function. Then we have a certain amount of satisfaction in ourselves which allows us freely, and without any attachment, to pursue other things in our lives. Whatever these things may be, we can do them or not do them. We can succeed, we can fail, but not one of them threatens our basic inner foundation. Established in that core, we have a degree of fulfillment that frees us from other levels of attachment. This allows us to work in a state of surrender in relationship to everything that we might ordinarily feel we have to accomplish in our lives.

From this perspective, there is no pressure to attain or accomplish; there is only an internal concern to do a good job—not because we seek praise, but rather for the simple satisfaction of doing. Then whatever we pursue is perfectly fine.

The point of a spiritual practice is to find the simple intensity of the stillness within ourselves, to cultivate our experience of that stillness, and not to let any of what goes through our brains distract us from it. What goes on in there is an endless merry-go-round of up and down for as long as we live, but we do have the choice not to get involved in the up-and-down part of it. There is, instead, the deeper part of us that is always present. We can engage in that anytime we choose by simply turning our attention toward it and trying to feel it.

We can do this if we concentrate for a little while and pay attention. When we do so, slowly that thing in the middle of our chest that we call a heart will start to open and function as we understand a heart should function. We can really start to feel and experience that we are alive. We can start to feel a new depth and a dimension to our lives that we each can recognize as authentic life.

Then, no matter what happens to us in the world, we feel we are having a truly rich experience. No matter what feedback the world gives us, we know that we have creative work to do. We have a foundation from which to do that work and rise above all the dissonance. Then we are nourished by life and able to give back to it in a real way.

The point is to stay established in the inner stillness at our core and to not set up a lot of entanglements that will operate as obstructions. Because attachments are tensions. If you think they're not, try to get out of one—then you will see tension.

The inner strength we establish through our inner work allows us to enter the world without any particular requirements or desires. Instead, what operates is a concern to unfold the creative power existing within us. This concern then keeps our attention on the flow of our own creative energy. It becomes the mechanism by which we are able to absorb the universe in ourselves.

TO LIVE

without

PURPOSE

I T SEEMS AS though everybody needs a reason for being alive. Some people make that reason earning money, others make it having love in a relationship, while still others make it into career or some way of helping the world. Everyone has a different reason. However, from a broader perspective, all these reasons are related to a finite sense of purpose—and no sense of purpose can be anything but finite.

What is called bondage is the limiting condition and source of all the suffering we experience in our lives. It is due to our attaching some purpose to our actions—meaning that we want some particular outcome to follow. This identification with a sense of purpose is the fundamental cause of our unhappiness. We act in the hope of that outcome, not seeing that it is fundamentally useless to do so.

In truth, we add nothing and take away from nothing. Why? Because in truth we are merely articulations of the vital force of Life Itself, and it is the nature of this vital force to express itself. But this is not the same thing as saying that it has a purpose.

We call this vital force the *Self*; it is the essence of all things. We can say that the Self has no purpose other than creative Self-expression. And if the Self has no purpose, then it has no inherent limitations—and certainly no problems. Those we make up ourselves. When we free ourselves from the notion of purpose, we are free to discover what we are. And that's very big.

⌐

To say that our lives have no purpose is not to say that they have no value. There is, after all, something deeply precious about them. However, as long as we operate from a sense of purpose, then there are all kinds of efforts we have to make, so many struggles in which we have to engage, so many different contests we have to undertake. As a result, we end up building tensions, barriers, and structures into our physical lives and our minds that have no foundation in any deeper reality. We set up a certain heaviness that denies us access to the well-being that lies within us all the time.

Our spiritual practice consists of training ourselves to keep our attention inside and focused on the energy of that vital force all the time. This is so that instead of becoming immersed in life's strain and struggle, we are always aware of the dimension of our lives that has no problem.

To be free from the burden of purpose in our lives enables us to have a very different viewpoint about any activity we undertake in the world. It doesn't deny the value of activity —as Krishna told Arjuna, we *must* act. We assume that activity is an unavoidable as well as an important and healthy part of our lives. However, instead of undertaking activity for the sake of some objective, it simply becomes an articulation of the creative potency of the energy itself. Instead of being limited by the confines of some problem that we defined, our effort is directed toward creating the possibility of finer and diverse ways in which this creative energy can express itself both in our own lives and in the other lives we touch. Instead of living a life that is a struggle for something—even the struggle for truth—we live a life that is fundamentally free.

This means that our lives are also fundamentally free of certainty. So, we had better get comfortable with this idea, and not many people are. Of course, death, taxes, and lawyers are still part of the picture, but our understanding of the whole becomes different. The real point is coming to understand that every outcome, without exception, will be uncertain. When we really face this fact, then we can live a life full of curiosity, enthusiasm, and wonder as the treasure in our innermost heart of hearts slowly unfolds and reveals its extraordinary content. Our only effort becomes one of cultivating this wonder toward Life Itself.

When we are free of a sense of purpose, we don't have to search for answers that are fundamentally irrelevant to our existence. We are free to live open to every situation that, at one time, we imagined to be a difficulty or a conflict. The various tensions we encounter, instead of representing reasons to become depressed or angry, become occasions to refine and deepen our understanding of this creative energy of Life Itself. Then the field of our activity becomes the canvas on which we, the artists, express the creative capacity of our essence. Our lives themselves become works of art.

⌁

The Baltimore Catechism of the Catholic church poses the question in its religious instruction, "Why did God make me?" The answer given is that "God made me to know, love, and serve Him in this world." Although this may seem simplistic, it is perfectly true. To know, love, and serve God is to exist in a purposeless state, totally open to the will of a higher power.

To be open in this way is to live in direct contact with the perpetual, dynamic uncertainty implicit in the power of Life Itself. This is the same thing as living in the heart of infinite freedom.

～

To say that Life has no purpose may sound depressing. And in some ways, it may be—if, in killing ourselves to invest tremendous energy in what we are doing, we discover that ultimately this gets us nowhere at all. On the other hand, to be free from the sense of purpose that usually operates as the motivating force behind our lives is an optimistic situation. It is, in fact, known as *Liberation*, freeing us from the compulsion to enact some dimension of our biological imperatives to eat and reproduce.

The fundamental cause of bondage is the sense of purpose we attach to our activities, due to the ways we identify with these biological imperatives. As long as these imperatives, in all of their expressions, govern our horizons, then we are going to experience a lot of disappointment, pain, and misunderstanding.

In fact, if we really want to get depressed, we can think seriously about our purpose in life as getting a job and making money. That means we get to stay here, work our brains out for fifty years, get our teeth kicked on some regular basis, after which we die. This is a profoundly limited option.

I am not saying that we don't have a responsibility to function well in the world. In fact, I insist that the people who study with me have jobs and cultivate as much skill as they possibly can in the context of their work in the world. We cannot understand the possibilities that present themselves to us when we really grow unless we have sharp and disciplined minds.

Moreover, living without purpose is a way of talking about awareness and freedom. It is not about living a life that is out of balance with the nourishment system of which we are a part. It is not an irresponsible attitude. Rather, it is a profoundly responsible attitude that not only allows us to be free, it also allows for the continuous freedom and release of those people to whom we are connected and with whom we share our lives.

Unless this is the case, somebody else's sense of purpose is going to conflict with ours, just as our respective desires are going to translate into a set of tensions we try to impose on somebody else. Then, one of us will start beating up on the other—and what's the point of that?

Whatever purpose we hold to should at least be continuously deeper than the level on which we are immediately functioning—and, at a certain point, we get to a place where there simply is no further need for purpose at all. When we understand the absolute fallibility of our bodies, minds, and emotions, our only conclusion can be that there must be something deeper than all that. When we pursue that deeper something, it becomes experientially clear that there is but one Self—and it has no purpose. The world is nothing but that, the vitality of which is the underlying reality of everything.

—

To say that life has no purpose is really a statement about the nature of the Divine. God is not up there with a faulty switchboard waiting to answer our calls and letters, and God is not waiting to choke Oral Roberts if he doesn't collect eight million dollars.

You and I have nothing we were sent here to accomplish. There is no reparation we need to perform. We are not sinners, we are not evil, and we are not here on the rock pile to work off so many years of bad karma because of something we did in a past life. We are neither here to resolve past misdeeds nor to do something at the request of some deity—particularly not to shake somebody else into thinking as we do. We are here simply to experience the joy of Life Itself and the joy of being. When we start from that point, then the different ways we find to express ourselves become arenas in which we can refine an awareness of that which is unchanging throughout all experience.

—

Illusions are the glue that holds a person together as an individual. I once saw a book that posited the value of illusions and, at least on one level, I had to agree with it completely. For life lived on that level, illusions are necessary. What else will function to keep a person together, to keep one organized and going?

However, what we often think we work for in this world is, in fact, an illusion. Implicit in the Bhagavad Gita is a discussion of attainment, non-attainment, and their fusion. Krishna continuously points out that it is better to work and it is essential to serve. If there is such a thing as sin, the greatest one is taking up a work and leaving it undone. I would add to this that spiritual work is a work that should not be left undone.

To enter into increasingly deeper levels of experience is to surrender our illusions. It is to release our orientation of purpose and to allow our whole lives to be sacrificed into the flow of infinite creative energy. Whether that means losing everything, giving up everything, or gaining everything is not the point. We cannot be concerned with what lies on the other side. To be concerned with what is on the other side is not to go at all.

⌒

Life Itself has facets within facets within facets. From the point of view of our involvement with the world, it is possible to say that we operate with goals and objectives. However, from the broadest possible perspective, our lives have no such purpose, no such goals or objectives. At some stage, we must have the ability to see this biggest possible picture without losing contact with the reality of the world in which we move around.

This is something like what a musician must do in giving a performance, during which there are many things to manage. The first thing is to have an overview of the piece one is performing—a sense of the parameters and of how much the spirit of the piece allows one to depart from the written music. The biggest possible view of the performance is important, but if that broad view causes the musician to forget the notes, then there is no piece and no real performance. In the same sense, if one's concern about each individual note is too great, then the piece has no spirit. It becomes just a loose expression of notes.

The highest understanding is established in the broadest possible point of view. At the same time, it never denies or departs from the specifics of the creative expression.

⌒

We cannot influence any pattern in our lives without letting go of it completely. That's the paradox. As long as we have any intention to influence an outcome, we have not released it. As long as we want—no matter how subtle that want may be—then our want is the central point from which we operate. This holds true all the way up to wanting to know God.

People always have many wants operating. That is what makes us so rich and complex. We are such creatures of want that even simple things like being hungry set up an intense inner vibration from which our mechanism speaks. Generally speaking, we then just want to respond to that vibration—to feed the system. Rarely do we take the time to observe the nature of the vibration itself. We don't use the hunger as an opportunity to understand our own essence and the dynamics at work in us. We don't let the vibration intensify and change, to reveal its subtler components. Were we to do so, we would begin to recognize the nature of wanting itself, independent of its particular forms.

⸺

As soon as Arjuna saw the long-term picture, he knew exactly what he had to do. In a way, this was very practical of him. Did this practicality represent any kind of limitation? No it did not. Rather, it functioned as a support.

When most people say "Be practical," they usually mean "Be limited." I am suggesting something different. In this case, to be practical means to be focused. Being practical is then just a matter of understanding how to carry out whatever it is we focus on doing. It is recognizing the various obstacles, giving the event an appropriate structure, and then articulating the whole.

—

To awaken our awareness of the vital force is to look inside ourselves in order to discover and cultivate the deeper aspects of what we are. To see the universe inside us is such a startling experience that, in some ways, it is like somebody suddenly turning on all the lights. It is amazing to have the tensions that bind our hearts and minds just let go so that we can take a breath and feel suddenly and completely alive to this reality within us. We suddenly know beyond intellect that this is our true reality. Then we say, "By God, you know, I am awake." But that energy was always there.

To feel free and alive in this way is the experience of vital force. And within that vital force itself, there is no inherent purpose. It simply is. The reason we pursue an awareness of this energy is to discover the depth of our own humanity and to begin to live from the awareness of that depth. In this way, it is possible for us to become established in an underlying state of total well-being.

—

The expression of Life Itself is nothing more than the throb of rapture of a primordial vital force. And that rapture has no purpose other than to experience itself. It is like this: If I'm walking down the street on a sunny morning and I'm feeling pretty good, I may start whistling or singing. What's the purpose of that? Maybe it's nothing more than a demonstration that I'm feeling good. That's all.

Likewise, the whole manifest universe is nothing but a demonstration that the infinite presence is permeated by a great joy. This is its highest characteristic. And when you are full of joy, what awareness of purpose do you have? None. When you are not, you become filled with the desire to create or recover that state of joy. This joy is greater than pleasure or pain. It exists at the point where pleasure and pain merge and become one.

~

Years ago, there was a television series called *Kung Fu*. In the episode, the teacher rolls out a great sheet of rice paper and says to the student, "You must learn to walk on this and leave no footprints." Only a person with no sense of purpose can do this. In this same way must we move through the world.

It is our nature to act, and no one lives without doing. But doing with an attitude of detachment affords us the greatest possibility of accomplishing what we set out to do in the first place, of enjoying what we are doing, and of leaving no footprints to mar the paper in the end.

Another way of saying this is that when we learn to quiet our minds, to free them from a preoccupation with purpose and outcomes, then the nature of the highest state becomes quietly clear to us. Just as in certain parts of the world we can look deep into the ocean on a calm day and see far down to the bottom, when the mind is quiet, the actual nature of our awareness becomes clear.

⌐

When we really understand our spiritual pursuit, we begin to see that the highest state of spirituality is one of pure openness. Krishnamurti uses the words "neither accept nor reject," calling this a state of choiceless awareness—choiceless because it is not fixed on any particular objective or purpose. It has no stake in any specific outcome to its actions. So, in spiritual work, we want to arrive at a state in which there is no purpose because purpose itself is limiting.

Choiceless awareness is not about deliberation or assessment. It is not a discipline or a habit, and it cannot be practiced. It is simply an alertness to the moment. It is an eternal presence, which is identical to the core of our very being. The whole range of complexity and sophistication that we are is a testimony to the creative power implicit in this eternal presence. But it cannot be said to have a purpose.

⌐

At a certain stage, even the idea of spiritual attainment reveals itself to be an illusion. This is a sophisticated line of thought that you may want to park and not come back to until you have enough experience to actually deal with it. I say this because it can be a somewhat dangerous line of inquiry that you have to be careful with. Still, even in the realm of spiritual work, there is nothing to attain.

As long as we have an objective, even if we try to define it in spiritual terms, we will always be at least two steps away from that attainment. The point is that the highest state is without purpose. In fact, at this stage, even the notion of growing becomes irrelevant. We simply are.

WE RISE

by that by which

WE FALL

ONE OF MY favorite sayings in the Buddhist scriptures called the *Hevajra Tantra* is: "A person rises by that by which they fall." This means that any external challenge has as much potential to lift us up as it does to throw us down. In the deepest sense, it means that the same crystallized energy that represents tension, stress, pain, and suffering—when released—has the potential to uplift us powerfully and to expand our awareness.

This particular Tantra suggests that the only real difference between up and down is in our understanding of a situation and our capacity to deal with it. A challenge either knocks us down or lifts us up, depending on our attitude, our awareness, and our orientation. If we are relating primarily to one of our biological imperatives, then every obstruction to that biological imperative will result in a further condensation of this biological cloud. This only causes us to become more and more identified in the limited, separate sense of what we are. This, in turn, strengthens our ego even more. This is what pulls us down.

Shakti is a Sanskrit term for energy or vital force. This energy is double-edged—either it can liberate or it can limit. What is resistance for a while, once penetrated, becomes support.

There is no such thing as positive and negative energy, or even positive and negative situations. Energy cuts both ways. Moreover, both support and resistance act as the source of all structure. What is an obstruction at one point can become a support at another. What in one form or relationship is not so good for us can be, from another angle, not so bad. What is at one point a resistance—once we are beyond it—can become a support because of the way we change our relationship to it.

In its proper place, nothing is a bad thing. When we are in the stillness in the middle, we can observe the shifts closer to one extreme and then closer to the other. It is like a pendulum. We want to find what the Buddha called "the middle way"—the stillness at the center.

Our real concern is the balance point, which is always a dynamic and continuously shifting event. It is not a rigid mental point of view. Only when our minds are like water—free and flowing—can we flow within ourselves and in the world. When this happens, the idea of the stillness at the center and its dynamic nature begins to make sense. Actually, it is as if we wake up to find our understanding of ourselves and the world in which we live changed.

This has been referred to as a kind of higher consciousness, but we could just as easily say that it is a matter of seeing things the way they really are. This is why truth is so elusive.

⟜

The way we change is by releasing the tensions within ourselves as we go through our day. We relax and open our hearts to everything. In a way, it is mindlessly simple—except, well, to go out and try to do it. I say this because we all create patterns in our lives that we invest with enormous importance. We invest so much energy in our ideas, our emotions, our personal histories that we have no chance of escaping the boundaries of that investment. Then we are dominated by them.

Even so, we can open our hearts and start to change ourselves whenever we want. We may not be completely transformed in fifteen minutes, but there will be times in our lives that we will identify as powerfully transforming periods.

During those times, in fifteen minutes, all kinds of things may go on. What happens in such periods is that pressure builds up for a long while and then gets released in a flash. The issue is how that release will be structured into the field of our experience and understanding. Will it be structured destructively or, because of our capacity to maintain our awareness and discipline, can we structure it into some creative or inspired experience? It is up to us. We each choose.

⌒

Whenever we frame an issue in terms of "this" or "that," we have defined it incorrectly from the start. We will only get a response that is inappropriate—because everything is always both this and that.

If what is at first resistance can also become a support, then every experience is like a double-edged sword. When we are neither attached to nor repelled by any experience, we become aware of each as a series of different cycles and sequences. Ultimately, they all reveal their contents to be creative energy. And every aspect of experience is a mixture. One minute we are saying that something is wonderful and that we want it. Then, when we have it, we look at it and say, "This is a drag. Get me out of here." We are all yo-yos that way—always shifting.

Better to see that, whatever we do, we are going to pay a price. We might as well know that on the front side. Everything costs. This includes growing as a person. It is not free—it costs. Indeed, it will cost us our lives. It will also give them back to us over and over again.

⌒

We look at the horrific images of certain Hindu deities and they seem completely ferocious. But if we look again, we see that these same deities are also full of sweetness. This is an intentional statement about the eyes through which we ourselves are gazing. For example, if we look along the lines that appear so fierce, suddenly the gentleness emerges. What has fangs and is glaring at us turns into an enormous grin and hairy eyebrows. Both appearances are present, that of foe and friend. Those who look casually see only the wrathful deity; those who look carefully will see a protector, a guide, a support. So, one function of these deities is to demonstrate the dual nature of the highest reality, which resolves into something beyond either pole.

In Hindu mythology, the gods and demons are brothers. For that matter, the god Rudra, who is the prototype of the god Shiva, is represented both as a demonic figure and as a healer. For example, a hymn to Rudra repeats, "Don't make us sick. Please don't kill us." Yet, at the same time, Rudra is the god who heals, the god with the medicine. In the same way, the hymns beg Rudra not to be angry and mentions in passing that he brings many blessings. In a single figure, Rudra embodies the tension inherent in saying that God includes everything. What we distinguish as demonic and divine are actually one.

Is it a contradiction to find in the essence of Life Itself what we would describe as both good and evil? If we see that divinity is invested with power in every direction and that all forms of experience extend from the Divine, what happens to our understanding of God? I suppose it is like asking where a Bengal tiger sleeps. Wanting God to do "good" things is like wanting to domesticate the Divine. This is not possible. So what does this say about a person who is immersed in an awareness of the Divine? How can you classify such a person?

In many Tibetan paintings, the gruesome and demonic creatures are meant to represent powerful internal and external energies. One being called *Mahakala* is Time—because time is ferocious and devours everything. Likewise, these ferocious creatures are also in the service of Truth; that is, they reveal the truth about everything. If we are ambivalent about our relationship to the truth, then they may seem horrific. If we have a firm conviction of our connection to the truth, then they become a power that supports us.

The issue we face is whether we are consuming our lives or being consumed by them. We could also say, whether our lives are happening from within us or happening to us. I would suggest that each of us is a vital field of energy from which our lives extend. I am not talking here about our bodies, minds, or emotions, but about the vitality preceding them all. The body, mind, and emotions are all effects of this vital field that we can call conscious energy, consciousness, or the energy of Life Itself.

If our lives are happening from within us, then the most important issue is whether or not the energy of this field is organized to support our growing. Are our lives an expression of real fulfillment or not? It is like any living phenomenon: If the full potential of the event is going to manifest, it will take all the intensity and strength of the organism.

A spiritual practice is intended to release us from being locked in our heads. We may not always want that release, but at least the alternative should be there for us. Granted, given the intense conditioning that most of us have received, the idea of being freed from living in our minds can seem frightening. What will we do, stripped of our mechanisms for classification and differentiation? How will we live if we are not thinking and thinking and thinking all the time about this or that, and especially about "What's going to happen to me?"

However, something wonderful happens when we begin to quiet our minds, open our hearts, and live from an entirely different level of our own vitality. This vitality does not attempt to classify, to grasp, or to understand anything intellectually because that kind of understanding is simply another way to classify.

Why do I challenge the value of classifying or categorizing our experience? Classifications give us mental structures through which we can operate and feel less insecure or adrift. They help us feel in some way connected to and in step with the things around us. However, as we discover through the practice of meditation, this is not the true nature of reality.

When we open ourselves through our practice, we start to bring our attention inside and keep it there. Slowly, with our breathing and concentration, we release the tensions within us. This opens deeper channels of creative energy and levels of creative awareness and expression. Slowly, our intellectual, emotional, and operational boundaries begin to dissolve.

In dissolving these boundaries, we recognize that all boundaries are superimposed and therefore subjective. That doesn't make them bad, but if they are subjective and if we have the opportunity to choose, we might want to get a sense of the real flavor and dynamic of our lives before we start setting up walls around different parts of it.

To engage in this conscious process leads to a transformation of our values. It allows for the possibility of bringing together our stated values and our manifest values. In other words, we operate in a way that comes much closer to our stated ideals. Moreover, because we end up with fewer tensions within us and create fewer tensions around us, the range of our capacity for creative expression is greatly extended.

⌐

In stillness there is no need to evaluate our own strength or weakness, because in stillness there is no such distinction. There is only divine light and the power of creative energy. From our contact with that subtle and powerful understanding, we can know, in the deepest sense, the state of our entire system and make no decision that complicates it.

For example, if you consider a situation by asking yourself what effect a given line of behavior will have on your mechanism and your inner work, it is not so difficult to discern the right decision. With a little patience, everything shows itself. It is only when we don't consider carefully that we lose a lot. This is not really all that hard, and it doesn't take genius. It just takes somebody who is at home with the lights on.

We choose whether an energy will become part of our resistance or whether it will support our growth. An example is the things we dislike about ourselves—what we think of as the limitations we are trying to get rid of. These are all energies with vibrations to them. In fact, when we encounter these conditions in ourselves, our reaction to them can sometimes have such a strong vibration of its own that it leaves us unable to act.

However, having concentrated carefully and worked to cultivate an understanding of that condition in order to master it, suddenly we discover that what we considered to be a problem is not a problem at all. Instead, we find that it has become a gift and even a talent. It was just a seed waiting to be cultivated. This means that what we are so busy trying to get rid of, beat down, and dissolve are really things that we should be investigating closer.

The fact of the matter is that attempting to do anything but continuously engage that highest state of pure awareness is, in a way, a useless struggle and a waste of time.

I don't think of anything as springing from impurity because all reality springs from the same source. This is the double-edged nature of the highest reality—it gives rise to what we think of as impure just as much as it does to what we imagine to be pure. So, at that level, what distinction can there be between impurity and this supreme nectar? Any distinction lies entirely in our perception.

In no way am I seeking to deny the fundamental reality that we are. Rather I wish to embrace it in its purer form. Purity in this context has nothing to do with any rules of behavior; it has everything to do with the absence of attachment. And absence of attachment means being utterly open to the reality of a situation just as it is. It means looking the truth of it dead in the eye and not closing our own eyes to that truth.

＊

Paradox persists because, when everything is contained in one thing, we cannot avoid any part of it. Day and night, light and darkness are one thing. Good is only possible to identify in the context of evil. The two lean on each other. This makes paradox not merely a convention of language, but a description of reality.

＊

If tension goes to tension, then any initial tension within us will be reflected in some aspect of our experience in the world. When we drop that tension, the nature of our worldly experience changes enormously.

The issue of emotional and intellectual baggage is certainly relevant in this discussion. But it is our ability to go to a new level—to integrate the paradoxes of a situation and see a higher resolution—that enables us to unfold the potential in that situation. If we try to work things as we think they ought to be worked, we only become frustrated, other people get tense, and things fall apart.

⌘

We are the pain as well as what cures the pain. And we are as close to Eternity at this moment as we will ever be. We taste that Eternity without knowing it, even at this very moment.

⌘

There is, in the world, no form of behavior that we need to avoid. Furthermore, I don't find repressive programs all that useful—especially in spiritual development. By setting up lists of do's and don'ts, they just create traps for people to fall into. Better to be clearly focused on the creative flow of vital force within ourselves. This will take us deeply into the core of our own being, into a state in which there is only a total well-being to which nothing can be added and from which nothing can be taken away. That clear, steady, lucid state contains the potential for every form of manifestation as well as the capacity to articulate every potential concept and feeling. In other words, there is no lack or limitation in it at all.

Entering that state, our lives become a process of Self-discovery because we don't know what we are going to find out there. The truth is that none of us knows, even though most of the time we tell ourselves that we do. We tell ourselves this by creating boundaries to enclose what we think we know. And when things don't go the way we expect, we work still harder to push whatever is happening back within the parameters that we are able to accept comfortably.

Of course, what we're really doing is slowly squeezing the vitality out of our lives as we reduce the dynamism in order to have what seems to be greater comfort and security. I'm not against comfort and security—but it has been my experience that lasting comfort and security exist only in that deeper state of total well-being.

Even the idea that there is good and bad action is part of the mistake. This basic blindness emerges when we begin to see things as one way or another, and we identify with the one and reject the other. This conditions us to perform in certain ways, expecting to be rewarded or punished.

This is not altogether surprising. From the earliest days of our parents attempting to train us, we learn that certain things bring us pleasure while others get us into a whole boatload of trouble. From there, we start to think in terms of right and wrong, of good and bad, instead of observing that fundamentally our lives flow from within us and fill up the entire field of our experience and awareness.

Ultimately, there is no separation between the most distant thing we can perceive and the deepest inner experience we can have. They are not separate experiences but different aspects of a single reality.

Part of our spiritual practice involves carefully examining any intense experience that we have. On the one hand, this includes anger, hatred, and violence—anything we generally think of as unpleasurable intensity or experience. On the other hand, it also includes our pleasurable experiences. Both give us the opportunity to gain insight into what transcends these individual circumstances and unites all poles of experience.

We could also call it, according to the Tantric notion, an infinite moment of purity. A pure person is one who functions in this state of non-attachment, widely and radically open to whatever direction the energy within a situation chooses to take. In this state, whatever we do is done from our experience of the highest reality within us—an experience that we cultivate through our meditation practice. This experience is at once intense and expansive, which is why different spiritual texts use the analogy of the fire, heat, and intensity of the Sun and the coolness and joy—the nectar, if you will—of the Moon. These are fused in a single state from which circumstances spontaneously arise, not because of some limited desire, but because of the vitality of Life Itself. Another analogy is of a flower with no particular desire that, on being nourished, unfolds and manifests great color and fragrance.

In this state, a person's view becomes one in which there is nothing that is not love, nothing that is not God. We discover that the ultimate giving is a simple joy that we feel within ourselves and extend throughout the whole universe. The ultimate religious act—in fact, the only authentic one—is simply the love of the whole. This recognition, despite how it may sound, is not a simple-minded assertion but the outcome of great attention and focus. Having it, we become stable and steady within ourselves, filled with the understanding that nothing can possibly be added to or subtracted from the fundamental condition of well-being that we are.

When we have the capacity to take in every experience as nourishment, freed from the fear of what is going to happen to us or any concern about living or dying, then we can grow through every experience without trying to locate it in some set of pre-existing categories. Experiences that awaken us are not divorced from ordinary life. It is, in fact, in the context of the ordinary that such occasions occur, and at any moment. This means that any event, however small it may seem, can become the occasion for our transformation into the fully Real.

In the process, we undergo every form of experience—from what we consider to be romantic, emotional, and in some way lovely and pleasant, to the brutal and violent, and even to forms that we are conditioned to consider perverted and disgusting. These various experiences in their totality become the different fragrances, colors, and textures of the bouquet that is the manifestation of Life Itself. Extended to the Infinite, the variety and vitality of this bouquet is the creative expression of Life Itself.

SURRENDER

THE BASIC PROBLEM for human beings is that, on one level, it appears as though we have some power. For instance, I can move a book from one side of the table to another and it will stay where I put it. I can move my body from place to place. I can rearrange the chairs in a room. This capacity gives us a sense that we can do things, that we have power.

The problem with this assumption is that the dimension on which it appears we can make things happen is limited in the bigger scheme of things. The rules of the game, as far as Earth is concerned—whether down to the dimension of molecules or out to the reaches of the solar system—may seem pretty extensive. Therefore, in the big picture we are really discussing a limited arena in the totality of manifestation.

We are actually composed of quadrillions of particles that do not operate according to the same rules by which we imagine we operate. In a quantum sense, there is no proof that human beings or even objects as we perceive them really exist. All classes of objects, such as galaxies and universes in space, exist and influence our lives dramatically on a daily basis. Yet it does not necessarily follow that these things operate by the same rules governing our everyday lives. Furthermore, our idea that we move things around and therefore have some power denies the fact that the real power to move things does not exist in the dimension of books, tables, or bodies. It emerges from an entirely different dimension.

To make a long story short, we are not nearly as powerful as we think we are. Likewise, the consequences of our actions are not as clear as we usually imagine. Within a limited time frame, we may be able to predict a few things in the behavior of a dynamic system, whether it be a person, a relationship, a social system, or even an eco-system. However, beyond a small prediction, we have no idea where a thing will end up, and outcomes in a larger sense are intrinsically impossible to anticipate.

So, the whole cause and effect cycle in which we live our everyday lives and orient a large part of our personal relationships and worldly activities is a lot less reliable than we like to think. The linear way we usually approach the issues in our lives—the things we worry about, the events that entangle us, our desires, fears, and aspirations—has limited real value and only ends up being the source of tremendous frustration for us. Therefore, it is necessary to rethink our actions, their outcomes, and the appropriate stance to take in relationship to both.

I would suggest that the stance be one of surrender. This may seem like an odd thing to say—after all, I've been talking about being the heroes of our own lives. And what does surrender have to do with being a hero? Well, in this case, surrender has nothing to do with giving up and everything to do with opening ourselves to a situation just as it is, allowing the creative energy inherent in the situation to unfold, and letting go of the attempt to control the outcome. Instead, we choose to do everything to support the creative unfolding. This is real surrender.

Krishna tells Arjuna in the Bhagavad Gita that, as a warrior, he has a single task: to surrender to what he must do. The outcome is not in his hands and he must not think about it. His job is to go out there and live or die according to the will of God. That is all.

The struggle to avoid death is futile. The fact is that, in one sense, it doesn't matter whether we live or die—because we constantly do both every day. The only real salvation is to accept death in all the little ways we die each day and prepare ourselves to face the bigger death at the end. At the same time, the continuous renewal happening within and around us borders on the miraculous.

Surrender, in any case, is the beginning and the end. As we surrender, throughout our whole field of experience we discover what I call the breath of God. It is our awareness of this breath of God that unites every separate event and every occasion of surrender. It is what gathers up our focus and allows us to be centered on what we are really doing in the midst of all the distinct events.

This necessarily means that we surrender all of our desires over and over again. In a sense, desires are not real anyway—they are only the wish list reflecting the limits of our imagination. Beyond the surrender of our desires, this commitment becomes the continuous sacrifice of our physical lives and egos into the creative flow of Life's unfolding from within Itself.

Our willingness to be open to Life's program allows us to serve Life wholeheartedly and without reservation. This gives our lives meaning as our existence enters into serving the only reality there is—the expression of Life's own creative energy. This is a service not only to ourselves but to others, precisely because it is a service to Life from which nothing is distinct. In this way, we find unity on all levels of Life and experience ourselves as whole people.

In every case, this understanding is what allows us to stop obstructing the program that Life has for Itself. It allows us to identify with and become established in that program so that we become the vehicles through which it unfolds. This is the nature of surrender.

First of all, we only surrender to ourselves—never to anything or anyone else. Secondly, in growing, we may discover things about ourselves that are a bit disquieting. In fact, I should hope that we would discover that we are not quite what we thought we were. If we were to keep seeing ourselves as just what we thought we were, then we would probably be dishonest with ourselves and not change all that much. I myself am not the person I would like to be—I am simply the person that I am.

We have to open our hearts every single day to the tensions within and around us and not get too involved in what we like and don't like—because it all changes. When we start getting into some kind of self-critical mode, better to forget about it. Do we loathe ourselves over the past? Life goes on. Do we loath the future? That's useless—because life turns on a dime. We may never win an Oscar or a beauty contest, and who cares? Ultimately we are all going to die. The people who get the recognition and the people who don't get the recognition all end up in the same place.

This may sound harsh, but I am trying to get at what is really important about our lives. As we move through these lives, we want to be in contact with the deepest possible place inside us. From that place, we evoke the greatest potential available to us. And we don't know where it will lead. If we did know, then there would be no point in the journey.

Dealing with tensions and learning that we can surrender and rise above them allows us to cultivate a deep trust in Life Itself. In turn, the strength of our trust makes it possible for there to emerge from within us a capacity to serve whatever situation we find ourselves in. This service is really the creative activity of connecting and weaving the inner and outer until they reveal themselves to be the fabric of the whole.

⌑

Even when we surrender, a situation can return. Changing our relationship to it doesn't mean that it will disappear. However, it does mean that the situation will no longer make us hysterical when we have to deal with it. We can rarely just walk away from anything altogether. If we haven't learned to be above something, it will keep coming back at us over and over again in one form or another.

There are two elements here. First of all, there are the situations in our lives that represent real challenges to our growth. These constitute about ten percent or less of the stress that we will ever experience. Secondly, the remaining ninety percent of the stress is our own fabrication. This automatically means that the odds are better than nine to one that if we drop our own tension about something, we are dropping something that was useless in the first place.

That leaves the real things we have to deal with—the ones that, if we don't deal with them, will come looking for us. We cannot run and hide, and there is no place to walk away from them because they will chase us. So, at some point, we have to stop and face them.

Most of us have our rationales for not doing and not doing and not doing. However, with things that keep coming back around, we finally just have to button up our guts and do them. The most central of these things is the inner work we have to do to grow as human beings. And this means letting go of what the world thinks of us—which includes our husband or wife, our lover, our children, our teacher, or anybody else. We have to be ourselves and do the best job we can.

Ultimately, we only have to live with ourselves and be able to face ourselves every day. That is what growing is about.

⌒

Surrender is more important to spiritual growth than any specific meditation technique. Surrender simply means relaxing deeply while being completely alert, discovering our center, and allowing our heart and mind, our guts, our sexuality, and every other part of us to become connected —so that we are a whole, complete event. As this inner connection takes place, we start to feel it gathering down the front as we draw our breath down. Then, as it all comes together, we start to feel it slowly rising up within us. We feel it moving up our spinal column as we exhale. This is called the rising of the kundalini energy, or vital force, and it is a meditation that we practice over and over again in order to feel the flow of vital force within us.

This rising up brings about an internal transformation of the vibration that we are, as it slowly becomes finer and finer. Allowing this connected energy to refine itself and begin to function within us is what transforms us. As we deeply relax and become aware of this energy rising up, we also become aware gradually of the various levels at work within us along with the varieties of dynamic manifestation taking place.

As this happens, we cease to be limited to the physical realm of experience. It no longer represents the confines of our reality. Instead, we experience ourselves more and more as a multidimensional event. Our awareness is extended enormously and we discover that we are not what we thought we were.

The key to this event is not technique. In fact, the key is not about *doing* anything. It is not a matter of whether we are doing enough or not doing enough. Forget about that. The key is to find the stillness in our center and learn to stay there. The "staying there" part is the surrender because, as we connect to that center, the internal re-wiring that happens will make us feel itchy and twitchy, on fire and agitated, irritable and irascible, and everything in between. In the face of all that, we will probably go through periods of feeling lonely, dejected, angry, and out of control—the whole range of feelings.

Surrender, however, is about just sitting through it all, letting go of every manifestation of the energy that comes up, and allowing it to slowly work its transforming power within us. If we can do that, then we discover a different network of energy that happens from within us, through us and around us and back again. Moreover, that energy was there all along—it was just shrouded over by the tensions in our system.

Our new awareness of this energy network dissolves the idea of the boundaries between objects. It changes our whole understanding of the dynamics in our field of experience. It makes us directly and palpably aware of the ultimate source of power and its effects.

When we find our center and learn to stay there, we allow the self-organizing, self-regulating, self-renewing capacity of Life to mobilize itself to the fullest. It only requires the ability to focus our minds on one thing—namely, our own deepest wish to grow—and to stay tuned into the process as it changes and changes.

The ability to sit still through this process has nothing to do with technique. Technique will give us some ways to relax and stay open; it will also give us some preliminary insight into stillness. But unless we have the resolve to know stillness deeply and to let go of all tensions that stand in the way of that knowing, then all the technique in the world will not amount to a pile of beans.

Surrender is the issue—discovering and articulating the power of surrender, and allowing that power to manifest in our lives. This takes commitment, devotion, and persever-ance. With these, we as human beings have every possibility of realizing our highest capacity.

Surrender is difficult to talk about. It's just something we do. And when we surrender everything, we discover that we haven't surrendered anything at all. In fact, the only thing we can really ever surrender is our tensions, tensions that I usually equate with our stupidity.

In one sense, we may hear ourselves thinking, "So, what do I have to give up? In which way will I be threatened? I'm not sure I can do this thing."

With all due respect, this kind of thinking is useless. What could be more wonderful than having the capacity to take a breath, feel our hearts open, and begin experiencing our own creative energy unfolding? What could be more exhilarating than feeling the liberation of releasing the tensions and burdens of our lives? As we experience that sense of release and relief, where do we turn our attention if not to whatever we naturally love and want to enjoy in a deeper way?

In some way, we are all trying to release one burden or another in order to have the capacity to love deeply and completely. What continuously obstructs us is our fear and insecurity, our shyness, our sense of inappropriateness—every kind of worry that makes us deeply contracted. From a position of surrender, however, deeply loving has no essential limitation. When we deeply love, we love free of attachment. Ultimately, love is oriented not toward one thing or another, but toward the Self within us and all things. In that sense, love is unbounded.

Surrender is not a heavy thing. It only gets heavy when our egos enter the picture. Then it seems to take on all kinds of serious overtones. But at its core, surrender is not serious at all. It is immensely powerful and, in a way, it is the ultimate act an individual can undertake. Still, it is at the same time a simple, joyous, and uncomplicated occasion. Only our entanglements make it seem limiting in any sense.

As long as we are highly conditioned individuals, a certain willfulness is implicit in our approach to life. To reorient that conditioning—to de-condition ourselves—also requires a certain amount of will. When our attention is totally externalized, it can take a lot of effort to internalize it— and even that is not so easy. For example, if you are a woman who happens to get PMS to beat the band, how much will is going to save you from the difficulty that you may experience or inadvertently inflict on others? You just have to surrender to it continuously. In the final analysis, no amount of will can get us where we need to go.

The relationship between will and surrender is this: We *will* ourselves to let go. This is much more difficult than willing ourselves to hold on—because willing ourselves to hold on comes naturally. However, it is also a complete illusion because the only thing we hold onto are our misunderstandings.

It is not that *"My* will should be done." It is that the will of God should be done. And that is only discovered in surrender, which has nothing to do with the way we want anything to go. That is, it has nothing to do with our egos.

It is not possible to have a clear idea in advance of the depth to which our egos function in our lives or the work that the deepest surrender requires. We only discover these things in the practice of surrender. Whether it is surrendering in what is potentially a wonderful situation or a difficult one isn't important. We ultimately encounter both kinds of circumstances in which we are called upon to give our lives. There will be situations in which we are sort of willing and others in which we definitely are not. It doesn't really matter. It only matters that we stay centered in our inner work and respond from that center.

If we maintain our own center, the energy of Life that is inherent in everything will manage itself better than we ever could. It is only when we are out of balance with ourselves that we start thinking things like, "How can I manage this energy? How can I manipulate it and control it?" In a state of imbalance we are concerned about control. In a state of balance we don't worry about control. The thought never arises. This is because we simply experience everything as a multiplicity of rhythms functioning in harmony with one another.

My teacher Rudi taught that you have to want to grow with your whole heart and soul. All of the mechanisms of the practice in which he trained his students were aimed at acquiring the deeply intense feeling of this wish to grow. As a person's yearning to grow matures, it becomes a profound love of God. It becomes a real passion to know Life, not as so many objects in the material world, but as the vitality that animates everything.

As we mature in this process, we notice that a shift occurs: Wanting to grow becomes the surrender of everything. This is what Rudi was teaching at the time of his death. He expressed it in a prayer: "I surrender everything—thought, form, matter, sound—everything."

Spiritual maturity emerges in people who surrender everything—their desires, ambitions, needs, every kind of tension and want. In releasing these aspects of their individuality, they are able to participate completely in the infinite variety of Life.

There is no meditation practice, nothing that we can do, that will allow us to arrive at that ultimate state of surrendering everything. Yet only in that ultimate state of surrender do we experience love—for what is love anyway but ultimate self-surrender? The amazing thing is that in that self-surrender we do not experience a depletion. This self-surrender brings a profound and total experience of renewal, and because of that we have value for love. It cannot be understood or analyzed; there is no message in it. It gives no support to any particular direction in our lives. Love is vast beyond all discussion of coming and going, up and down, or right and left.

We have spiritual practices and teachers to nourish and support us until we come to a point where we simply, and from within ourselves, can release everything. It is in that complete release that Universal Love reveals itself to our minds and through our bodies into the world. There is nothing more important than the experience of that love.

Surrender is difficult because it is only surrender when we do it for its own sake. It can have no other purpose, no program, no reward, no object. It survives and flourishes in an environment in which there is no attachment to the outcome of our activity, but only a general participation in the total ecology of the situation.

⌇

Only when we let go of all the worries and fears about our lives and begin instead to trust in our own infinite inner Self is it possible for that inner Self to unfold. That's the only way we can come to any kind of real understanding about it. Otherwise, the patterns of tension that manifest as our minds and emotions, by their very existence, constantly attract us to certain things and repel us from others. They thereby completely structure and limit the way we understand ourselves and the world as well as the way we articulate our lives.

The rhythm of our lives is always going to change, oscillating between dynamic and still. To attain a state of well-being is to be established in a state in which dynamism and stillness are equally present. Sometimes the emphasis will be on one thing, sometimes on the other. Sometimes we will be more quiet and introverted, sometimes more extroverted. There is no real need to think much about that or to make any value judgments about the particular character of our lives at any given time.

Ultimately, we surrender everything. To be able to do this, our energy and attention must be directed inward. It is as though we were performers on a stage. Even with an audience to relate to, ideally we are also articulating something of substance from within us. To all the world, because we are performing for an audience, our behavior appears exactly as that of anyone outwardly oriented. But, in truth, what we are really communicating simply expresses itself because of the depth of our practice and our focus on the creative substance within us.

In this experience of surrender, there is certainly the possibility that we will encounter what the Spanish mystic Saint John of the Cross wrote about as the dark night of the soul—when our illusions fall away and we have nothing with which to replace them. We will experience things that will distress and frighten us. This is because entering into a deeper pattern of energy—a more profound cycle of the creative power of Life—can be frightening. This is represented in various mandalas, which really signify energy patterns. At each of the mandalic gates is a ferocious-looking gatekeeper, just like the fierce guardians at the entrance to many temples in India.

These guardians represent the emotion or chemistry that arises within us as we confront the possibility of experiencing a more profound power at work within us and our lives. Just as an example, have you ever noticed how falling in love can be one of the most frightening things that can happen to you? To learn about surrender also means learning to face fear and sit through it. There is no way around this if we wish to grow.

Basically, we are talking about work, some of which may not leave us feeling all that sweet. Yet the state of surrender has its own kind of satisfaction, regardless of whether we feel sweetness. There is a kind of righteousness about it. To give an analogy, when I play tennis, all I care about is hitting the ball well. I truly don't care if I win. At the same time, I don't feel all that much sweetness from hitting the ball well when somebody else is beating the pants off me. When we are hitting the ball really well and still find the other guy pounding it back in our faces, that is not about sweetness. Still, we can walk away feeling a real satisfaction in the experience.

When I think about enthusiasm vis-a-vis things of the world, I think of the enthusiasm of soldiers on a battlefield—of all the young warriors who have been fed tales of the valor, glory, and riches that come from war. They practice for long hours only to get out on the battlefield and find the honor and dignity of their code, training, and conduct disintegrate into a mass of blood, intestines, and shit flying all over the place. The reality of war is forever different from the propaganda about war—and this is basically true of everything.

This is why it is important to keep our attention inside ourselves and to move through life awake to its reality instead of succumbing to the various illusions that present themselves. Whatever job we do may be less than inspiring. However, if we engage in it in a spirit of surrender, we lift ourselves up to a different level of experience.

In that state of surrender there is neither room for enthusiasm nor falling back. There is only room for being centered. This is when we have the possibility to experience the subtle, deep satisfaction that comes from maintaining our center and functioning from our own deepest resource.

I think that is why the discussion in the Bhagavad Gita was set in the context of a battlefield. It is why Kashmir Shaivism often use the terms "hero" and "warrior." These refer to the spiritual hero, the spirituality of the warrior.

Surrender is a deeply sacred act. It is one in which effort and no effort, action and inaction, are fused. In every sense, it should uplift us, free us, and release us from our delusions—hopefully, before they hit bankruptcy. Nobody can compel anybody else to surrender. It is something that we can only do for ourselves. But in the face of absolute truth, surrender is the only appropriate response. It is the only thing we can do.

The

CREMATION
GROUND

AT THE END of the fighting, the battlefield becomes the cremation ground.

Among the ancient yogis, hermits, and renunciates of India, there was a practice which, to some extent, still exists. These people would carry on their meditation practices in the cremation grounds where the bodies of the dead were burned. Not surprisingly, the more orthodox society of India found such practices impure and beyond redemption.

Because of the stigma attached to death in Hindu society, nobody with any social standing got involved with dead bodies, with the food offered to the dead, or with the accoutrements of the rites. Contact with anything dealing with corpses was considered completely polluting. So, those who went to live in the cremation ground could never return to their earlier position in the social order. It was a serious step to take.

People went into the cremation grounds in order to pursue power. It was not a power implicit in the place itself, but one that they discovered by entering those parts of themselves that went beyond psychological experience and emotional events. They entered the cremation ground to gather up their own vital force and, as they recognized the ephemeral nature of their bodies and of experience in general, they reached into a larger whole.

In the mythology of Kashmir Shaivism, a whole set of images developed around the god Shiva and the penance he had to do for killing Brahma, the Creator. Shiva repented, but to demonstrate his repentance, he had to live for eons in the cremation grounds as Aghora Shiva. He never bathed or cut his hair. He went naked and smeared the grease and ash of the burnt corpses over his body. His devotees, the

Aghora Shaivites, meditated while seated on corpses in the dead of the moonless night.

To go through such an experience puts a person entirely outside the norms and conventions of society. At the same time, it reorganizes a person's whole perception and understanding of those norms. In Brahmin culture, for example, contact with the dead is the most disgusting thing that can happen to a person—not to mention contact with wine, meat, and the by-products of sexual intercourse. To confront what one finds most frightening and horrifying and to go beyond that fear and the horror creates an extraordinary possibility for freedom. It can open a person to the experience of a deeper well-being that exists within, independent of surrounding circumstances. This makes for a tremendously powerful person.

The cremation ground relativizes every other experience. It suggests that everything we think we value gets left at the gate. It is the place where all human endeavor comes to its natural end. In many ways, this is also what Krishna showed Arjuna when he revealed his fully divine form. As Arjuna watched, the thousands of warriors on the battlefield—those very people whom Arjuna had refused to fight—were swept into Krishna's mouth and devoured, all taken back into the Divine. This made clear to Arjuna that all the toil, the struggle, the suffering, and the pain that human beings endure take everyone to the same place.

Krishna's revelation pointed to the fundamental futility of any pursuit as an end in itself. This same idea was also expressed in other more horrific poetry, which was intended to remind the reader of where the things we think to be of value ultimately end up:

> A wretched ghost tears and tears the skin,
> then eats first the flesh, strong and putrid,
> that being thick or swollen is easiest to get:
> the shoulders, buttocks, and the backflesh;
> then drawing out the tendons, guts, and eyes,
> he bares his teeth and from the corpse upon his lap
> calmly eats the remnant down to the marrow in its bones.[4]

The cremation ground and all the orgiastic symbolism and activity that took place within it was a direct challenge to everything a person was likely to hold onto about his or her individuality. For some people, it functioned as a test; for others, it was simply a living demonstration of their liberation. For those for whom it was a test, the question was whether or not they could sustain a simple, joyous stance, even as they entered the cremation ground filled with the stench of burning bodies and littered with the residue of skulls, bones, and grease scavenged by dogs. Could they go there in the dark of the moon and stay simple and open?

---

[4] Daniel Ingalls, trans., *Sanskrit Poetry of Vidyakra's "Treasury"* (Cambridge: The Belknap Press of Harvard University Press, 1965, 1968), poem 1530.

Imagine the fear of entering such a place, where you would join with others in drinking from a skull, eating forbidden meat, drinking alcohol, and engaging in sexual rituals. On the one hand, there was the fear of a situation from which one might want to withdraw and couldn't; on the other hand, there were things in which one might want to lose oneself but couldn't. This is because the real issue was not in the doing. It was in how you extended yourself and whether or not you got entangled in it.

A kind of brain-breaking tension happened. You were put in a situation where you had only one choice. You couldn't withdraw and you couldn't get entangled, so you had to walk a razor's edge of pure balance and total harmony. This experience was calculated to elevate you beyond every kind of duality. It aimed to challenge every one of your biological imperatives as well as your sense of survival and your emotional need to be secure. It forced you to confront what your hormones made you do and how you behaved when they kicked in. If you were able to come through it, you began to transcend the whole realm of duality, of attraction and aversion, and all value judgment, all the psychology and the need to analyze anything. Instead, you simply established yourself in a state of joyous surrender. In this experience lay a tremendous power:

> The carrion-eater dances:
> he produces day and night by successive opening

and closing of his eyes;
he covers heaven with his quill-like hair that flies in
all directions.
He drinks the downpour of the clouds that streams
from the openings of the skull he holds within
his hands.
He breaks our eardrums with his mighty roar.[5]

In the iconography of Tantric art, you will see people cov-
ered with ash, with three lines on their foreheads, and with
their hair piled on top of their heads. They carry tridents
with skulls and wear strings of finger bones around their
necks and the skins of animals around their waists. The
skins are for sitting on during meditation. These people
also carry skull-cups to eat their meals from. This was an
asceticism that diverged from the forms of purity one
sometimes associates with the renunciate.

Of the people living in the cremation grounds, undoubted-
ly some were crazed. Yet among them were also some extraordinary people who chose to step outside the framework of
the established social setup in order to fulfill a true spiritual
impulse. Recognizing the superficiality of what they had
been doing in their lives, they ventured into the cremation
ground.

---

[5] *Sanskrit Poetry*, Ingalls, poem 1541.

For these people, nothing was disgusting. Instead, everything was beautiful. The point of having the gods enter into them was that everything then became godly. Smearing themselves with the ashes of dead bodies was a way of confronting others with their own reactions to the disgusting. It was intended to force a recognition that the surface of all life ends in the disgusting, while the life within it is pure and compellingly vital.

⚊

There is nothing gentle about the imagery of the cremation ground. The smell of burning flesh, the sound of bones exploding in the fire, and the light cast through the dark smoke is unforgettable. The iconography of the gods is terrifying as well. In fact, Bhairava, a name of Shiva, is another term for terror.

In one sense, all of the Tantras are concerned with the pursuit of power. These people, however, recognized that power cuts two ways. On one level, power serves to fulfill our desires. In doing so, it also makes further work for us to do, because even when we acquire the things we want, the path of liberation still lies before us. On the other level, there is the path to liberation itself. This path, if pursued, puts an end to every issue related to the ego and our individuality because it takes us into the core of what we are—a place that lies beyond finite individuality.

I often use the term "infinite uncertainty" to refer to what we feel when we begin to put aside the "busy-ness" and all the tensions in order to relate directly to the core of what we are. Infinite uncertainty is what we feel when we start to recognize the superficiality of what we cling to as our lives. It is the sense of terror we feel underneath our mind and emotions—the sense of fear and insecurity—that compels us to ask in different ways, "But what's going to happen to me?" That terror is considered to be Bhairava. It is the anxiety a person feels in entering the cremation ground and confronting the end of life—because what happens in the cremation ground is that body after body goes in, and nobody comes out alive.

To enter the cremation ground is to confront everything we fear. This is not only our own demise, but also the possibility of living without support. After all, the people who lived in the cremation ground survived on the food offered to the dead. Of course, if they got really hungry they might go wandering with a skull-cup until they came to someone's door. They would then say, "The rays are hungry." The energies are hungry. The living dead are hungry.

Yet these people were not malevolent or particularly against anything. They simply stood beyond, outside, above everything. No social conventions bound them or held meaning for them. They entered such circumstances to become strong.

They had no ambition, no desire, no need for recognition. There was nothing to accomplish, no work to do, no aim except to recognize and participate in the fundamental power of Life Itself manifesting in them.

It is frightening to stop thinking of all the things we pursue as important in order to go out and simply live. But it was in this environment, free of desire, delusion, and attachment, that these people discovered what it meant to recognize and participate in the vital force of Life Itself, of which our body, senses, and intellect are all a manifestation. Such an experience compelled them to recognize the infinite potential that lay within them.

And this is not easy. To cut through all the layers often feels worse before it feels better. This is because our tensions operate as the different mechanisms by which we attempt to map out and defend some territory. As the identity that we have struggled to build up starts to unwind, we feel the ground shiver with the question, "What's going to happen to me?"

Anyone who has undergone transforming experiences or engaged in any creative process recognizes both the terror and the joy that alternately pulsate through us as we confront the uncertainty within ourselves. This is the only place where uncertainty exists. Yet, in becoming stabilized in the fluctuation of that terror and joy, we discover that both are permeated by a state that is more subtle and that pervades the two.

—

By the time it was being described in the old texts, the experience of the cremation ground had been absorbed into the daily life of some of the learned Brahmins. The people who wrote these texts actually went out into the cremation grounds to perform these rituals, although some performed only a stylized or mental reenactment. In either case, these writers were not actually cremation-ground ascetics. Why, after all, would a cremation-ground dweller care about recording anything at all?

Generally speaking, the authors of this material were Brahmins who lived under royal patronage, often holding some position at court. They didn't see themselves as radicals reacting against society. On the surface, they looked and acted like anybody else. They fit in. They acknowledged the structures and pathways of the world as real and respected the sensitivities of the people around them.

They conducted their ritual and spiritual lives in private. These practitioners didn't go out and share what they were doing with everybody. They recognized that, for most of the world, the expansion of power results in increased suffering and violence—not in the experience of ultimate reality. They understood that one must be steadfast in one's resolve to become established in ultimate reality if one is to pass through such experiences protected and unscathed. But at that point, *all* experience becomes an extraordinary source of power by which we are nourished and through which we are transformed.

—

These practitioners considered no experience wrong or bad. We would not have gotten them to accept a maxim such as "Do no harm," because the very notion of harm from their larger point of view was meaningless. It would be like Krishna saying, "What harm are you worried about causing? I give life and I take it back. Who has been harmed by what? Life arises and subsides in me, and everything in between exists only in me. So what harm can you cause? It is I who am and do everything."

Looking at life this way does not mean we cease to have concern for other people's feelings or that we give up respecting each other. These things are necessary to sustain the essential balance in our everyday lives. However, the Kashmir Shaivite tradition denies no experience its validity. All experience arises from the same field and has the same power, the same constituents, the same essence.

Even so, these people lived in such places as a continual reminder to themselves of life's ephemeral nature and of the finitude of our physical existence. In this way, they reflected upon what, exactly, the power of Life is that moves and motivates everything. Furthermore, it served to remind them about the nature of ambition, attainment, and responsibility.

Ultimately, the end of any accomplishment—even the most refined spiritual work—is the cremation ground. It is the end of all power and all manifestation. Therefore, those who lived there neither bothered about such things nor were all that impressed by them.

In India, the analogy of the cremation ground is used continuously as a metaphor for transformation. It is symbolic of the commitment to a self-sacrifice that is also a process of total transformation.

In one sense, we are burning up our lives in a fire that we have initiated within ourselves through our spiritual practice. The image of the cremation ground says that the distinction between living and dying is an artificial one. If we are really going to live, we must in some way surrender ourselves to a depth that essentially embraces death and then transcends it. To achieve that, we must be willing to lose everything, to give everything up. Then it is not a loss but an accomplishment.

The color orange is the color of fire. It symbolizes both the fire of the creative process and the fire that continuously engulfs the physical form. The renunciates who wore robes of orange were thus wearing this fire at all times. Today, the orange robe of the swami signifies the cremation fire to which one has given over one's life. This is not such an uncommon notion in different religious traditions. For example, Catholic priests wear black because it is the color of the shroud and a way of representing that the person has died to the bondage of the world.

In our spiritual practice, it is essential for each of us to recreate the cremation ground for ourselves. If we are serious about becoming free in our lives, we are forced at some point to go over the edge—to undertake a great act of surrender. This amounts to a profound leap of faith. At some point, something happens that forces us to let go of our attachment to everything we ever did, everything we ever thought, and all the momentum, effort, work, and development we ever imagined we were creating. We are forced to give up everything we thought we had done and everything we thought we were, discovering in the process that the reasons we thought we had for doing these things now seem ridiculous.

Yes, it's scary. And, yes, you ask over and over, "What's going to happen to me?" However, for the part of us that is preoccupied with that question, the answer will be found in the cremation ground—that place where all our earthly pursuits finally carry us.

We can have no illusions about the world because the world is essentially a trash compactor. A person has to be pretty agile to avoid being compressed by the pressures of living in it. Otherwise, these pressures will pack us down more and more densely, leaving us with little capacity for self-awareness. In worldly terms, our fate is already sealed. From a certain perspective, we are already dead—it's only a matter of when. This is just a truck stop and, in the biggest possible picture, the food we get here isn't all that much better than what a person gets at any truck stop.

If we operate from this perspective, we stop expecting the people and things in our lives to give us something they cannot. Then the work we do and the actions in which we engage are not done out of a sense of obligation—whether to our parents, ancestors, or society at large. We continue to act, but differently, out of a sense of love, appreciation, admiration, and joy—a real respect for life.

We don't need to reject the world. We need to learn to release and surrender it. In that surrender, we allow a total shift of values to take place and free us from desire, ambition, and even hope. Only when free from these things are we free to simultaneously participate in that non-reducible, indivisible, infinite dynamic stillness that is the essence of our very existence.

Some people are disturbed when I talk about ending desire, ambition, and hope. But on entering the cremation ground, who radiates hope? When one experiences the wholeness and fullness that comes from transcending the limitations of our individuality as systems of mind, emotions, and biology, then hope is no longer an issue. Instead, our attention turns to that which is fully alive in us then and there.

⟳

There is a kind of cremation ground within each of us. We don't need to do any particular dance to gather its power, nor do we need to go into any actual place—except the one between our own two ears. There, we take the tensions we find, release them back into raw creative energy, and create out of them a fire that will deeply transform us. That fire will liberate the power of love within us to nurture and free ourselves and everyone in our lives. It will free our inner vital force, resolving all of the debts, obligations, and entanglements we have ever experienced. It will free us to participate in the essence of our own lives—the energy of Life Itself.

⟳

The deeper meaning of renunciation is subtle. What we renounce are not objects or relationships, but being possessed in some way by the desire for and attachment to these objects and relationships. We do not renounce actions. Rather, we give up our attachment to the outcome of our actions—our need to have things turn out in particular ways. This is true renunciation. And understanding it frees us—because the objects and relationships in our lives have no further power over us.

We can now engage these things differently. We don't participate out of fear or greed because there is nothing to want and nothing not to want. Nor do we suffer the delusion that something is to be gained by doing these things. There is only the endless awareness of and wonder in the extraordinary power of Life—a creative mystery continuously unfolding itself. Then, as Abhinavagupta, the tenth century Shaivite sage, says, "Happily, just as you are, enjoy your own universal nature."

This means something subtle and powerful. The cremation ground, the sacrifice, the cremation fire are analogies for the release of our finite individual lives. Through this sacrifice, we begin to liberate the underlying vital force of our lives. We discover the infinite potential that permeates and transcends every thought, every form, every sound.

—

Within the great mystery that is Life, we own nothing. What is this competition we feel then, before we each go, one at a time, through the same gate?

It is to this cremation ground that those of us wishing to enter the experience of spirit are called—to this cremation ground which, in one sense, is horrific and terrifying, a place where not many people will follow. Still, all of our impressions notwithstanding, it is not a morbid place. Rather, it represents only the end of what is finite about us. It represents our freedom from the confines of that finiteness. To go there freely and without fear, openly releasing ourselves into the experience of Life Itself, awakens us to the awareness of our essence.

The

SACRIFICE

F

ROM TIME immemorial, people have sacrificed to God. The purpose of the sacrifice has always been to re-establish the continuity of the relationship and harmony between heaven and earth. The intermediary between the two has always been human beings.

People understood sacrifice to be the essence of the ultimate universal process. By sacrificing, a person participated in that process. This is the most sophisticated view: We sacrifice not to an individual god, but to the whole universe, which itself is nothing but an infinite giving of itself in sacrifice.

So, in the ritual of sacrifice, we reenact the world process, bringing this cosmic event into our surroundings, participating in it, and reenacting it.

In certain groups within the larger Shaivite tradition of Kashmir there evolved sacrificial rites involving the transgression of various social rules and prohibitions in a ritual context. This was done in the pursuit of absolute freedom and inner power. Particular rituals were carried out by those who went to live in the cremation grounds. Over time, the concept of the cremation ground was brought into the world of the courtier and the householder.

This was accomplished primarily by two systems of Shaivism, the Trika and the Krama, of which the latter was the wilder and more intense. Krama practices in particular characterized life as a cremation ground, and the rituals with forbidden things were more than a metaphor. These people were the extremists—the Hell's Angels of the spiritual realm—who had acquired the power of their own souls and who lived above and beyond all boundaries. Together, the Trika and the Krama systems comprised the Kaula tradition. Kaulism involved rituals that, in one way or another, made use of substances considered to be impure. It did so for the purpose of acquiring power and thereby liberation.

Abhinavagupta, a major contributor to Kashmir Shaivite thought, in the tenth century cautioned practitioners of these rituals not to violate the social and political structures of the day. On the contrary, he said only ignorant people wore their colors externally or were disrespectful of local mores. The marks of one's initiation and participation were not for show, and practitioners were neither criminals nor outlaws. They understood their society's rules clearly and, in a real sense, lived within them.

However, in their heart of hearts and the deepest core of their own awareness, practitioners were free of all such things. They came together and practiced their rituals to demonstrate respect for the totality of life in all its forms and of their contact with its highest form. Such people had an eye for what was real and simply appreciated it. They had no fear of death, of loving, or of life.

It is certainly possible that in some of these rituals, in their most extreme forms, the participants consumed human flesh. Certainly the poetry about the cremation ground suggests that this was so. But in its symbolic enactment, the event really concerned the consumption of ignorance.

The point is that consuming ignorance is repugnant to anyone. Who wants to have to swallow it? This is true whether we are talking about eating our own tensions or those of others. It is never a great pleasure. However, to do so transforms our understanding. As a result, we go beyond our individuality and its ordinary relationship role with the world into a sense of Self that transcends the paradox of life and death. This is the paradox of living in the cremation ground.

In the world of the Krama, rituals were significant because people's lives were so intensely structured. This was especially true of the Brahmin caste where breaking their strong conditioning required equally strong measures.

Strong structures in the West are different. We are trained to focus on becoming independent—on becoming "somebody." Therefore, the social and cultural mechanisms supporting this focus are best broken down by living simple lives in which service is a basic component and in which we learn what it means to extend ourselves. This is our form of society. The more we understand this, the more potent our experience of the deeper reality becomes.

On every level of our physical lives, ritual and sacrifice play an important role between us and the people with whom we maintain relationships of any kind. When we greet each other, it is a ritual. Different kinds of gatherings are also different rituals. In college, there was always the person who performed the ritual function of taking off his or her clothes, and then there was the person who got completely drunk and threw up his or her guts. Such activities, albeit superficial, confirmed certain kinds of relationship. We may have a hard time understanding the cremation ground rituals but, on the other hand, Americans conduct rituals all the time in which meat, alcohol, and sex are involved. After all, what else is a barbecue?

In other contexts, exchanging gifts at holidays and festivals is a way we give of ourselves in order to confirm and continue very different kinds of relationship. Giving things is the smallest part of any ritual. In the cremation ground rituals, while offerings were made of meat, wine, and other things, the most challenging part was to give of oneself. The rituals required one to dig intensely into oneself in ways calculated to confront all of a person's deepest instincts and inhibitions. They demanded that one evoke the capacity to change one's state and to extend the horizons of one's awareness. In so doing, a person had to shift the equilibrium of one's own boundaries. In other words, the rituals called upon a person to alter every cognitive pattern and habit for the sake of expanding the range of one's awareness within a greater field of function. This was a much bigger way of thinking about sacrifice.

My own feeling is that the ritual use of meat, alcohol, or sex was intended to evoke every kind of intense response. Even though the texts deny it, the Kaula tradition comes along and says, "In order to be a free person, you have to go through these things and look at them for what they are. You have to deal with them maturely and, in so learning, perhaps you will rise above and get past them." Or perhaps you won't. This holds true of drugs, sex, alcohol, or power because they are all forms of intoxication.

In the process of this endeavor, a person ultimately acquires some power and has to learn to deal with it. Those people who acquire power and attempt to use it generally discover that it is an expensive form of intoxication indeed—in which case it becomes all the clearer that surrender is the key to liberation.

The problem with power is that when we have it, we try to use it. When we fail, we think we are losing it, and then we try to hold onto it even more tightly, and so on and so on. The thrust of Trika and Krama rituals was to get people to recognize that power existed independently within them and had its own program. This is in the same sense that the fundamental life power within you is not something that you engender or sustain or make do anything. It simply *is*.

These rituals were a conscious and deliberate attempt to assault people's sensibilities and to turn the logic of their ordinary human endeavors on its head. They were also aimed at supporting people as they exposed themselves to every aspect of human behavior and every facet of life, from the violent to the perverse to the utterly mundane. At the same time, there was something pleasurable woven throughout it all. The whole point was to bring people to a degree of stability within themselves that would enable them to exist independent of any kind of circumstance in a state of peace, filled with a deeper experience of total well-being.

In our own practice, we learn to savor and relish the substance of all experience, whether it be anger, fear, sexuality, attraction, or aversion. All of it, without exception, becomes part of a mix of flavors. It is this great banquet that we consume and that makes us strong.

An essential part of the consumption and absorption of all experience into ourselves is the recognition of the superficiality of the notion of "other." If all reality emerges from the energy of Life Itself, what other can there truly be?

—

Think of the act of giving flowers to someone as a simple way to please and delight them. Remember your own pleasure in receiving such a gift. Is there not a kind of sweetness that permeates both the giving and receiving? Ultimately, the real gift is not so much the flowers as it is the exchange of sweetness you experience when you open your heart and feel that flow within yourself. As Krishna tells Arjuna, if done with an open heart, even the offering of a single flower is a gift pleasing to the Divine because that is the source of the sweetness.

The point of the different offerings in Tantric rituals was, on one level, to engage a person's senses, passions, and desires. At the same time, they were also intended to move one to look deeply into the core of all those separate experiences, to discover the single powerful energy at work in all of them. In taking one's attention from the object to the source, one came into a contact with the deepest part of oneself—that same sweetness.

Ultimately, we find that the source of all true richness—of all that we refer to as quality, pleasure, or satisfaction—comes from within us. We don't have to strain for it to express itself. In fact, it is possible that any strain we exert to acquire something in our lives actually operates at the expense of our true inner wealth—and not in its support. It may be that the price of strain brings something in the short term that is tremendously detrimental in the long run.

For me, wherever I sit in meditation becomes the sacrificial fire pit. The sacrificial wood is my breath. The sacrifice is my awareness of myself, which I burn up in my conscious effort and concentration. This rises into the heavenly sphere and provokes a response from the Divine in the outpouring of creative energy.

This is the process by which sacrifices have been carried out from the beginning of time, regardless of their form and regardless of the particular tradition or culture.

~

Real sacrifice is not one in which we offer something and expect something in return. Real sacrifice is one in which we offer up our whole lives—individuality, capabilities, allegiances—into the fire of our inner awakening and unfolding conscious energy so that we can be transformed as human beings. Intellectual, emotional, and material boundaries dissolve. This allows us to recognize our essence to be nothing but infinite spirit, identical to that spirit from which all forms of experience have emerged.

We can't stay the same and grow. We simply can't. So, casting ourselves into this fire, we hold to only one thing—the quality of our devotion and love. In fact, the only way that this transformation can take place and establish us in a higher order of our own spirit is through this devotion.

Without it, what happens? When we can't hold to this quality of love, then as real transformation begins we become scattered and unable to sustain the change. It turns into a bout of hysteria at best and a psychotic episode at worst. In casting ourselves into this event without love or devotion, we end up lower than the point from which we started out.

In real sacrifice, we offer up our hopes and fears, our desires and illusions. What emerges from that release is a clear, pragmatic vision of the nature of the world and individual existence and the capacity for discrimination based upon that clear vision. This capacity is profound indeed. Furthermore, this sacrifice brings about an inner harmony and serenity that only comes from a recognition of the infinite fullness of spirit at the core of our existence.

Greedy people seek to hold what they have and acquire more. The discriminating person recognizes that everything in life flows from that fullness of spirit. For those who attain the serenity and well-being that flows from that discrimination, life is nothing but a demonstration of the infinite fullness of spirit.

Without loving and devoted service, there is no experience of spirit upon which to build any recognition or to develop any discrimination. There can only be a cynicism based upon our worldly struggle, ambition, and greed. Anybody who has attained anything has attained it through the fullness of spirit manifest in his or her life. It doesn't happen any other way.

This is not a cold intellectual reality but an event of great heat, life, and awareness. It is surrendering the fruits and outcomes of our actions so that these actions are born of love and devotion and aimed at the highest best interest of the whole. This is the fusion of action and renunciation, and the fulfillment of our potential as human beings. It is what Krishna wanted Arjuna to understand.

It is neither sacrifice nor service if we expect any quid pro quo. It is sacrifice and service only if it is born of love—the love of Life Itself or of God. This must be the foundation of our spiritual work.

～

Life's creative energy unfolds from within itself. There is nothing to add to it and nothing to get from it. Within us—whether we are aware of it or not—there is a need to give. This arises from the need to allow this creative power to flow so that it can unfold its highest potentiality.

Like the notion of casting bread upon the waters—first we give, and then we receive. This is not in the personalized sense of "I'll give to you and you'll give back to me." That is business. Rather, we allow our own creative energy to flow in whatever direction is possible and necessary for it to do so. In whatever way we can give, we give and, in this way, discover that we get back.

This is not because somebody comes and gives us something, but because the giving itself is the expansion and extension of our own creative power. The greatest treasure, Life Itself, is what we are. As we allow that life to flow within us and from us in every direction, we are increasingly and infinitely enriched. This enrichment, in turn, has the effect of putting an end to the limited concepts we have of ourselves as individuals. It allows us to rest in our individualized experience of a far greater awareness.

~

Why is it that we feel the energy of life as love? The ancients looked at the sun and understood that the sun only gives. It is because of its energy that life on earth arises. Yet what does the earth give back to the sun? Nothing at all. Year after year, eon after eon, the sun pours forth its energy, makes our existence possible, and gets nothing in return. This is selfless service.

This is an analogy for the experience of love—the willingness to do when no self-interest is involved—that human beings occasionally experience. Love is our word for it. God, if you choose this concept, is continuously pouring forth and getting nothing back in return.

Think of it like this: Love is really giving of oneself from that state in which it is impossible to add or subtract anything and from which, even in the giving, there is no diminishing of the source. So, human beings would say that God is Love—or that Love is God.

We may not exactly know our own source, although we can easily see that there is some source independent of our individuality upon which our individual existence depends. Religion in some way or another attempts to define that source. In contrast, spiritual teachings essentially argue that to know or define it intellectually is impossible and even useless. What we should do instead is be a part of it, be attuned to it, be aware of it.

Beyond that, all thoughts and ideas about that source have no power as far as it is concerned. Nor are they really relevant to how we act out our lives. What is relevant is our contact and interchange with that source—the communion. This is the essence and the outcome of sacrifice.

The essence of liberation is a change in our self-identity. We no longer think of our individuality in the same way. At the same time, of course, we continue to operate through our bodies. We could liken this to the instrument we play in the symphony of Life. The music is not a piece that we cook up but a part that we are given to play.

Our changing sense of identity evolves from "I'm doing this," "I'm feeling this," "I have to do this," (accompanied by related assumptions of importance) to recognizing that whatever song we play is really the song of God. Our actions are really the actions of the creative energy. This balance and harmony of the forces within and without lead to a different sensibility. This change of identity is a profound and sacred experience that is examined by every contemplative tradition.

Our new way of thinking about ourselves is accompanied by a new respect for life. This respect is in the form of taking care of ourselves and the connections in our lives, realizing that they are as important as the veins in our bodies. They are lines of interchange by which we form part of a larger body, and the nourishment that comes to us along these lines is important. We respect the unity in all of life and understand that what we do to others is also what we do to ourselves.

When I talk about the unity of life, I don't mean that everything is the same thing. Life's essential oneness does not mean that you and I are the same person or that we should confuse our roles. After all, what would happen if everybody in the orchestra thought that he or she was identical to everyone else, and the violinist started reading the percussionist's part? It wouldn't work. We have to respect the differences and not just the unity of life.

People who do not recognize this common essence generally operate from a selfish base that causes them to do harm to themselves and to others. They spin a web of tension that reinforces differences and distinctions. It doesn't matter if I come from the sweetest, most open place in the whole world. If my intentions are perfect but my actions are a muddle, the net effect will be a muddle. Remember the old proverb: The road to hell is paved with good intentions.

The point is to be aware of and serve the highest, best interest of the whole. A great work of art or a great symphony—anything that is truly sublime in its genius—serves everybody at the same time with an economy of effort and motion. It serves the highest ideal and the most practical need, operating at the same time within the context of practical limitations.

To perform the true sacrifice, we have to operate from a base of authentic love and respect. The onus for doing so is entirely on us, regardless of what other people do. The issue is our own performance. My teacher Rudi used to say that if we really wish to grow, we have to see ourselves as possibly wrong, because how else can we absorb the information that will allow us to change? This is in direct contrast to many of the self-help notions floating around, especially the ones that tell you to think in totally optimistic terms. "Think you can do anything and think that you are wonderful."

There *is* a wonderful part to each of us—as well as at least two hundred pounds of psychic toxic waste burying that wonderful part. It is necessary for us to learn to draw nourishment into the core of all that—into what is wonderful—and slowly cultivate it and allow it to emerge. This will happen as we operate in an environment of love and respect. It requires an attitude of service, which in no way depreciates us. Rather, it uplifts everybody because we are clear-headed, practical, and coming from an understanding of the unity of life.

Our service releases something inside us that allows a flow to take place. This flow then extends itself and releases something in another person, then in another, and then in yet another, entering many different environments and working on many different scales. It operates to release tensions and to free the creative potential within everyone concerned.

When we can do this, we understand more and more that the real sacrifice is our detachment from the rewards of our endeavors. In a simple and pragmatic way, it is the process of allowing our attainments to flow, even as we continually reinvest ourselves in cultivating our own authentic life. This is what allows us to recognize our own infinite source.

⌒

What we are doing is giving of ourselves. If we are not giving ourselves to another person or to God, we are sacrificing ourselves into ourselves. In other words, we are sacrificing our small self in order to realize our higher Self. Every time the small self dies, it is like the death of a weed. It gives the higher Self a little more space to rise up and flower.

⟜

It is an interesting and peculiar circumstance that the last part of the *sannyas* ceremony in India, which is the ceremony in which one becomes a swami, involves renouncing renunciation. This includes renouncing the vows made during the ceremony itself. One holds onto nothing whatsoever.

This is a subtle point. However, if our goal is absolute freedom, then at some stage we will have to renounce absolutely everything—even renunciation and liberation. It is fine to have liberation as a goal, just as it is a good thing to do work in our lives. Indeed, one of Rudi's insights was that work is an important part of what we must do. As our understanding of ourselves and our inner work becomes more sophisticated, we recognize that there is increasingly nothing but the simple and endless sacrifice of ourselves and of the unfoldment of our lives.

This is because love is not "goal" oriented. Love is simply love. So, when we talk about spiritual goals, it is necessary that we not fall into some kind of stupor about what our spiritual work really is. It is necessary to be alert and engaged in the process of sacrificing ourselves—because we cannot be loving human beings unconsciously. We cannot be devoted or give or surrender—and be unconscious. A trance is not a conscious state. A trance is only a trance, a condition in which some other state or pattern is functioning in and through us.

Ambition and goal orientation deny us the opportunity to understand this. When we are ambitious and engaged in acting out our attachments, we do not pay attention to what is happening around us. We do not listen to and absorb the information that is implicit in whatever is in front of our very faces.

Loving authentically is loving with no other objective. If it *does* have some other objective, it is no longer loving and we are only back in business. Businesses need goals. In fact, without goals, businesses become disorganized, inefficient, and a waste. And, on a certain level, in our lives it is a good thing to have goals. Nonetheless, to achieve the highest state requires openness and flow as well as the capacity for endless self-sacrifice into the power of Life Itself. Nothing is higher. After that, what unfolds is an ever-increasing understanding.

We do our inner work to develop the capacity for this loving sacrifice—to cultivate our ability to know what it is and then to hold to it. In knowing it and in holding to it, we develop a capacity for observation and detail that is both subtle and powerful. What interests us is our concern for Life.

⤙

If we are ever to develop as loving human beings, we must have the ability to love and serve as consciously and as completely as we can. If we can't let go of our own trips, if we don't see how our egos obstruct us, if we're unable to recognize the potential that lies beyond ego and the power of that potential—then how will we appreciate the benefit that exists in growing? Without the ability to connect to and sustain this flow of energy, where will we find the strength and courage to overcome our own suffering or even to address any kind of suffering at all? How is it possible?

Renunciation and self-sacrifice are profoundly important. Those who are able to give of themselves absolutely are those who overcome the limitations of the circumstances into which they have been born. A person who is able to live a life of sacrifice is one who can overcome any of the mistakes or misfortunes that occur to him or her.

If we don't practice this attitude in an ongoing way, our response to the whole idea of sacrifice will be one of enormous resistance. If we don't cultivate this understanding ahead of time, we will find it difficult to do it when we hit the actual moment. It is hard to come up with it on demand because we are apt to see only a loss. We would have no experience of or trust in the power of love within us. And without that faith, we would only experience loss and resistance to the perceived loss.

On the other hand, possessing this trust, we endlessly discover and rediscover the infinite potential within ourselves and within the loving environment that we sustain. This environment has no object, no attachment, no goal. Still, it continues to unfold for the benefit of the whole.

DEATH

and

REBIRTH

IN HIS WRITINGS, Rudi refers to an experience that he calls death and rebirth. He describes it as a situation in which we experience ourselves as vulnerable in many ways—physically, emotionally, and mentally, for example—and during which our energy seems quite low. During such times, it is easy to think that something is going wrong. What is actually happening, however, is that as we go more deeply into the experience of service and sacrifice, our general vitality sometimes retreats in order to bring about an internal reorganization. As this goes on, we may find that we simultaneously seem to attract every kind of problem in our business, relationships, health, and so on.

The most natural response would seem to be to try to address all of these problems. But the more we struggle to sustain some external situation, the more we expend energy that could be used to facilitate the reorganization trying to happen on a deeper level. The real way to facilitate this deeper process is through surrender. In surrendering, we simply accept this lower level of functioning as the thing occurring at the moment. Because we elect not to worry about it or to struggle—because we basically open to the circumstance, become quiet, and attend to our own reorganization—then it can take place. What can come forth from us at that point is a much stronger and more vital person.

⌣

Think of the challenge facing Arjuna. His question was: "What is the right thing to do?" He wondered what line of behavior really would manifest truth and harmony to the highest degree under circumstances of such enormous compression and challenge. Krishna's response was: "Do what you are trained to do. Do your work. As I am the giver and the taker of everything, the beginning and the end, then in your own work there is no real gain or loss. There is only me."

We can think about spiritual practice in terms of the integrating of a person. Likewise, we can understand the experience of death and rebirth as a process of integration. People's lives usually consist of contradictions: what they think they are and what they are, what they say they want and what they really want, and then what they are doing about it all. Spiritual practice is a process that integrates these different aspects of a person by bringing us down into our simplest and most basic condition.

Every person has a number of personalities that emerge under different circumstances. We can think of spiritual work as a process of integrating all of those personalities, enabling them to communicate more closely with each other so that the information from one aspect of our existence flows into all of the other aspects. This reduces the degree to which we deceive ourselves. As we require less and less energy to sustain our multiple selves, the inefficiencies in our creative energy are reduced. We become clearer about who we are and what we are capable of doing.

Death and rebirth experiences are important in this integration process. As we go beyond certain boundaries and find more immediate communication beginning to take place between us, our own resource, and our different facets, then we see how entire lines of behavior simply dissolve.

Usually, the conscious mind is not in contact with the various lines of behavior it engenders—for instance, our fears, desires, or illusions. We don't automatically recognize these things as coming from a more superficial part of ourselves. In a period of intense integration, it is possible that lines of manifestation including relationships and aspects of our material existence may simply drop away. This may be a good thing.

It is not merely that such things become unnecessary— because they were never necessary in the first place. In this process of integration, it is as though they lose their vascular support. The psychic arteries, veins, and capillaries that extend from us to support them simply dry up.

They dry up because of shifts in our inner mechanism. It is not as if they have been cut off—although anyone who has had a big emotional investment in some event will certainly feel that way. What really happens is that the ego goes into a state of total disturbance for a while. Gradually, however, our ability to operate from a deeper inner resource makes that disturbance beside the point.

For the most part, people find it extremely difficult to endure the ego disruption that accompanies the process of integration. Quite reasonably, the ego comes up with every way imaginable to shout more loudly, "But what's going to happen to me?" As Krishna points out to Arjuna, this question appears first as a cup of sorrow only to be revealed as the cup of fulfillment. Similarly, the process of ego-fulfillment (or disintegration) looks wonderful at first but eventually proves to taste bitter. This was understood by the dwellers in the cremation ground.

—

It is not always easy to recognize that this process of death and rebirth is what we are going through. In our inner work, as in everything else, we usually work to facilitate some end state that we imagine should be the outcome. Therefore, we are more likely to pay attention to where we think we are trying to go rather than to observe and try to understand what is going on right then and there.

If we feel that everything is sliding away from us, we generally think we are somehow failing in our spiritual practice. So, we respond by trying harder. In trying harder, we put out more energy and fail to hear the more subtle signals going on within us. Trying harder actually functions to block out the very information that would help us to understand what we are undergoing.

Obviously, not every failure or loss can be ascribed to what I call death and rebirth. The process I am discussing refers to the total life pattern—not just to individual patterns in certain situations. Having said that, however, I must add that when we notice a general shift and decline in our energy and find that relationships that at one point supported us begin to slide away for no apparent reason, we can suspect that something is up.

Generally speaking, nothing can be done in such situations. We can simply know that our lives are undergoing a total change and be willing to release everything we are attached to. Most of all, we must expect nothing and hold onto absolutely zero.

Situations like these only come about at all because we have a depth of dedication and a maturity of commitment to our own growth. This is what enables us to release all of our attachments, exist in the void that remains, and allow everything to fall away as we wait. Indeed, all we *can* do is wait until the circumstances change and a new pattern starts to emerge. Even then, we have to be careful: It is easy at any point along the continuum to derail a pure circumstance trying to take place by mixing it up with some desire.

As this process unfolds, we find that all kinds of unusual physics occur in our relationships and activities. For instance, the support and interaction we expect from certain people will seem to evaporate. Or, in what was a harmonious pattern of relationships, the timing is suddenly all wrong and there is little real communication anymore. Once this kind of pullback starts to happen, it tends to continue. We find that the people we depended upon are now distracted and doing other things.

We also find that there is a tendency for all kinds of illusions to blow into our lives, particularly in the form of great attractions or great fears and difficulties. Every kind of extremely pleasant or unpleasant possibility is likely to track us down—and both are illusions.

We will feel like running away from some and running headlong into others. Neither is the right course of action. Instead, we must cultivate our ability to stay focused and let our lives change as *they* want to change—not as *we* might want them to change. We have to be simple about that and allow our lives to reveal themselves. Otherwise, we end up feeding our illusions and starving our reality.

Better to keep steady in the face of every kind of torment, sustaining ourselves in the void being created and trusting that a total transformation of our inner system is going on.

⌇

Once we see the path to take, we cannot vacillate about going in that direction. To have some understanding about a change that is necessary and not make it is like sticking ourselves in the stomach with a knife. We only demonstrate to ourselves how much we are not to be trusted. When we clearly know that there is a better way to do something and yet fail to respond, we only reinforce the negative attitudes we already carry about ourselves. We prevent any deeper strength and understanding from coming forth. This is the same thing as undermining a hundred years worth of effort. It is further complicated by the guilt, justifications, and defensiveness that invariably follow that kind of failure.

We work hard and come to a point where we face great uncertainty. A change is about to happen and we have no idea where we are going. Always in the time in-between, when one thing is dying and another is coming up, there emerges a space where fear, anxiety, and the pain of separation can enter. That is the point where we get to play fifty-two card pickup—where we just have to take a stand and let the chips fall where they may. The more relaxed we are about it, the less we will be tortured by the images, shadows, and initial vibrations that establish themselves within the vacuum created by whatever is leaving.

We have to understand and not be terrorized by the changes that are trying to take place in our lives. We have to learn to allow change to happen. We have to understand that, in every instance, pain is a manifestation of something beneficial trying to assert itself within the field of our awareness. We also have to clearly see that the cure for the pain is in the pain.

We can see how the Bhagavad Gita is also a discussion about death and rebirth. The Arjuna who goes into the battle is not the Arjuna who will emerge from it. His level of existence is transformed. In the process, his teachers and mentors, his cousins and brothers are all killed; some are revealed as terrible people while others are shown to be solid human beings.

A genuine transformation takes place, initiated and brought to completion in Krishna. The issue is not particularly one of Krishna as guru, but rather of Arjuna's inner practice and the revelation of Krishna's ultimate form of that practice. That is the story's real focus—not the battlefield and the things happening in front of Arjuna, some which involve him and some which are peripheral to his existence. All of it, however, transforms and uplifts him. This is enormously difficult for him as a person.

In our lives, we will find that only by facing difficulty with real determination to grow do we discover who we are and what we are doing here. Only when we have the ability to stay quiet, centered, and direct in the face of life's major transitions, undistracted by things that come to attract or terrify us do we have the possibility to engage in the deepest experience of ourselves.

This is what happens to Arjuna. Ultimately, Krishna is nothing but the very soul of the soul of Arjuna. While they appear to be connected person to person, it is not that at all.

———

The experience of death and rebirth often leaves us feeling as though we are undergoing a massive internal eruption. We may feel as though we are being split open and ripped into pieces. Such total transformation of our system can look like a nervous breakdown. The fact of the matter is that, unless we have the ability to take it into the next phase, it *is* a kind of nervous breakdown—which is why some regard the practice of Tantric yoga as potentially dangerous. So, the ability to stay simple in the midst of it is crucial.

We have to be thoughtful about this situation because it is difficult to intellectualize it. My general observation is that these death and rebirth changes take place primarily when a person is making a conscious effort to grow spiritually. They seem to be associated with dramatic and unforeseen shifts in the person's life pattern which tend to provoke unusual behavior or an exaggerated emotional response.

At such times, it is important to remember that God has not thrown us to the wolves. God is within us always as the essence of our lives. As we cultivate our awareness of this essence, more and more we understand it to be the power of our intellect, the source of our strength, and the joy that resides in our hearts. If we turn our attention there and slowly experience these things, all our doubts and fears dissolve.

The thing that causes people the most fear is their ultimate destruction or death. Yet does fear of dying change the reality of the situation one bit? Did anybody who was scared of dying ever get out of it? We know that physical life is temporary. And since we already know how the story turns out, we might as well enjoy the ride. Only by enjoying the experience as we pass through it will we have the chance to really comprehend what lies behind its temporariness.

It is better not to worry and instead to cultivate within ourselves our capacity to stay open and to feel whatever happiness we can. If we see things that get in the way of our ability to be happy, we get a broom and sweep them out. What is the broom? Our breath. We breathe deeply and this sweeps the mind clear. Then all of this energy, which on one level runs amok and frightens us, becomes the source of tremendous stability, sensitivity, and happiness. Then there is no fear, even though we still may face circumstances of great difficulty.

If we find ourselves in a situation where someone is swinging a sword in our face, the most essential and powerful issue is the one of how to face our own death. If we have time for intellectual questions after that, fine.

⌒

The real death taking place is the death of certain attachments. Non-attachment is the lived-through manifestation of surrender. That doesn't just mean non-attachment to material things, but to everything. It requires us to have the capacity to live continuously at peace with total uncertainty. The point is, of course, that we live in total uncertainty already. This is nothing new. Our tensions are therefore simply our attempt to hold onto something and to create some certainty for ourselves. Yet, in creating something certain, we deny ourselves access to our great inner treasure. We do not see that we are only holding onto rabbit pellets.

I talk about surrender because it is essential to have the ability to live at peace and with complete composure in the face of a truly awesome uncertainty. This cuts both ways. When I say "truly awesome," I refer to its destructive capacity. But the extraordinary thing about this kind of destruction is that it is also continuously clearing away every kind of crystallization and obstruction within us, creating the opportunity for the spontaneous expression of new potential.

There is no such thing as a loss, really. There is only endless transformation. Only our little minds call something lost because it changes shape. When we have the ability to sustain our composure during times of uncertainty, we will appreciate the elegant and beautiful power of Life Itself in all its forms.

—

Our real spiritual practice is to have the kind of internal control that enables us to move into areas that would otherwise cause us to panic—and still not panic. It is what allows us to go slowly, our attention on the values we are trying to express and the attitude we want to have in dealing with a given event. It enables us to go through that event with awareness about why we are there and what we are doing. It enables us to get to work—to become connected to the situation and forget about whatever insecurity we may have felt in the beginning. Instead, we simply allow to unfold whatever is there for us to do. Or we say, "This is one of those things I can afford to keep moving right on through." Authentic spiritual practice is therefore not about controlling our environment or anyone around us. It is about learning to discipline ourselves.

Each piece of work that our lives bring us is a chance to be buried or a chance to be free. It is a chance to die or a chance to be reborn. It is dirt that will either cover our coffins or create mountains rising above the clouds. We make of it what we will.

In a real way, our personal lives are endlessly being created and destroyed. This can happen as often as every breath—and it certainly happens every day. When we wake up in the morning, whatever was yesterday is no more and a new life is still to be created. Even though there is certain structural consistency, a change also takes place so that we can almost feel born again each day.

This implies that every time we come into an intense period, we will probably feel that our whole life is being undone and that everything we are is being dismantled. A sense of superficiality and temporariness will probably permeate whatever we are involved in, accompanied by a certain amount of anguish to go along with both the insight into our own performance and the concern over what comes next—how all of this will fall away and what will be left.

During times of death and rebirth, most people see nothing but emptiness and bleakness. Yet there always follows a recreative aspect to this process. And the fusion between the destruction and the creation, whether in our individual experience or on a more transcendent level, is inspiration.

GRACE

EVERYBODY WALKS
around with grace in their life. There is no person in whose
life it is not present. Indeed, our very existence is an expression of grace. The problem is that we don't recognize what
it is, we don't know how to connect to it and, even after we
have connected to it, we usually don't have the skill to sustain the connection.

Loosely speaking, the vital force of Life Itself has two
states: crystallization and flow. Yet it is still one thing, in two
different conditions. Grace is what we call that condition

when suddenly something appears to come out of nothing. What really happens, though, is that because we surrender—because we consciously or even inadvertently release some tension and open ourselves to the situation—suddenly energy resources appear and patterns are transformed. A sudden surge of vitality becomes available to us. We look around from that change in our own inner state and discover that our view of our horizons is now quite different.

From our biological perspective, we have little real choice in our lives beyond the activities related to eating and reproducing. This is what makes the whole question of effort and non-effort in relation to growing such an interesting one: What, in fact, does take us beyond the dictates of that biological program? To use slightly different language, there are gaps in the programming, and it is those gaps that we take advantage of. By recognizing the fundamental electronics at the core of the program, we develop the potential both to dissolve the programming, and to recognize that the disk itself is part of a system much larger than we had imagined.

After a lot of hard work to master the various strategies of a spiritual practice, we arrive at a stage where we recognize that, in a real way, we have no hope of *doing* anything further to bring about an awakening within us. Working harder is simply impossible. We even enter a kind of dark period as we realize that there is nothing we can do—and that it has been that way all along. There is only surrendering ourselves into stillness—and that is where we meet up with grace.

⌒

Talking about surrendering ourselves into stillness raises an interesting question: Is it that *we* have remembered stillness and thus entered into it, or has stillness remembered *us* and tapped us on the shoulder to say, "Here I am"...?

My own feeling in this matter is that ultimately it is stillness that comes for us, asserting its presence, compelling our attention and recognition. I find this perspective the most likely because of the degree to which our biological imperatives ordinarily cloud our take on things. This is why many people go through life with little if any conscious contact with stillness.

So, here is where we come to the question of grace. Why is it that stillness taps *you* on the shoulder, and not somebody else? Or, more to the point, if stillness is tapping everyone on the shoulder all the time, what is it that moves you to listen and someone else to ignore it?

What role does effort play in the whole event? I would say that while effort tills the soil, what makes the real difference is our capacity for surrender. In other words, love and devotion are the key. Beyond this, there is little to say about grace.

Looking back on my own experience, I can only conclude that there is some force at work that I haven't the words to describe. There is something within us that is moving us. Given the choices, I don't think that many of us have the sense to pick ourselves up out of the soup in which we live and move toward something finer and deeper on our own. Indeed, I think that this is probably the last choice that most people grab hold of. So, there is some force, something that stirs within us independent of our will, that only becomes an active presence in our lives when we will ourselves to surrender.

Interestingly, this something continues to stir no matter how many times we stomp on it, no matter how many ways we bend, twist, and shred it. It continues to compel us to want to know and understand it. It is not exactly that we do this, but rather that this thing within us moves us to know it.

It is one's passion for living and growing. It is not a passion that we choose. Rather, it is simply there, its depth and breadth to discover on a daily basis. Can we say that we choose any of this? Only in the sense that we make the choice to keep turning back toward it—to keep exploring and cultivating that vital force—instead of turning our backs on it.

Any discovery process is largely a matter of will, work, a lot of grace, and no small amount of surrender. We all have any number of illusions about who we are, what we can do, and where we are going. Moving along through the world, mostly we discover that *we* are not what we thought we were, *they* are not who we thought they were, and *it* is not what we thought it was.

What does that do to us? It either makes us deeply disturbed—or deeply happy and free. Some people become cynical and unhappy because their illusions are gone and lament, "Oh, what has my life done to me?" But others look at that same situation and say, "Okay, I was wrong. So where is the truth?"

That is where grace comes in. What is it that causes us to recognize when we have been doing something that is not quite right and to start looking for the shift? Many people continue to do the disharmonious thing until they self-destruct. Others don't. So, what subtle inspiration makes the difference? This is difficult to say. In spiritual practice, one works deeply and one works a lot. And grace enters.

The reason we think "spontaneous" when referring to grace or to any kind of deep, intuitive perception is because they exist beyond the realm of time and space. They are always spontaneous because they occur in infinity.

⌒

If we enter any situation mentally, philosophically, or emotionally inflexible, this inflexibility becomes a point of weakness that ultimately denies us access to the highest reality. Likewise, people who have no capacity to serve deny themselves access to that reality by this rigidity.

In this context, what is grace? Grace is service. It is both serving God and being served by God. To say this is nothing other than to describe the self-liberating, self-actualizing creative energy of Life Itself.

INTEGRATION

WHAT IF WE had a mechanism whose fundamental tendency was toward integration but which, because of various stresses and strains within the system, was unable to fully manifest that state? Suppose we released some of these strains, thereby allowing the mechanism to extend its range of function. What would happen? Naturally it would move toward integration.

If we had to do one thing to bring this about, it would be to surrender. However, ultimately the surrender would have to extend throughout the whole field of our lives all the way to the end. We would not just surrender this pain or that tension, but adopt a fundamental stance toward our lives as a whole.

—

The Bhagavad Gita considers surrender to be the most sacred act a human being can manifest. Integration becomes apparent through surrender. It may seem, perhaps, that surrender and integration are really two ways of talking about the same thing. However, I use the term "integration" in a much broader sense than "surrender." While a state of complete surrender is also a state of complete integration, the active part of surrender that we constantly experience is smaller.

In the simplest sense, surrender is the process in which we actively release our desires and attachments on a moment-by-moment basis. We take our attention out of our heads and let go of whatever turbulence exists in our hearts. This frees the energy stuck there to move throughout our entire mechanism. This is a means of purifying ourselves—of making ourselves into a very big vessel.

—

This universal integration does not proceed from our everyday life outward, but from our everyday life inward. Having a spiritual life is making the effort to integrate our ordinary lives more and more deeply into the flow of our own creative energy as it unfolds to reveal its highest potential. We simultaneously integrate our inner work into our everyday lives, and vice versa.

It is not exactly about acquiring some higher state of consciousness. I find that whole concept burdensome. I would say, instead, that it is about acquiring *ourselves*—recognizing, intensifying, and extending our own vitality to its absolute potential. This vitality turns out to be unbounded, infinite, and free. To do this we don't have to go anyplace. We simply have to surrender a lot, and look again and again and again with real eyes every time. We have to look and feel and discriminate, which means using our brains and our senses. Ours is not a spiritual practice that denies the importance of the intellect or the value of the senses. Rather, it is a practice in which we turn the senses and the intellect back upon themselves in order to recognize their real nature and go beyond their limits.

It means that we observe the dynamics at work between ourselves and other people. We really look at other people and feel them. By continuously taking our attention back and forth from our own inner flow of vital force to its extension into the various circumstances and people around us, we experience an internal process of integration throughout the whole field of our awareness.

Keep in mind that Life Itself is whole. It is one thing. Whatever differentiation emerges from within it, it is still one thing. Think about your own experience with lots of different kinds of feelings. Some surge up in you and motivate you; others smack you down. Still, these impulses— either to do or not to do, to reach out or pull back—all exist in that one field of your own awareness. While many things may appear to be happening, they are all expressions of you. Life's multiple expressions are fundamentally all aspects of one vital force.

Having this perspective is neither nihilistic nor a denial of distinct experiences. Rather, it is just the recognition that we find our own essence functioning in all forms of manifestation. One reason to practice meditation daily is so that every cell of our bodies can become permeated with this direct experience of unity and integration.

The people living in the cremation grounds, to some degree, engaged in a kind of possession. They had gone beyond shamanism because a shaman, even though he or she may live outside social norms and even the physical community, still plays an intricate role in the life of that community.

Even though shamans may leave their bodies and fly through the ether, that flying establishes a kind of contact and continuity between the community, the gods, and spirits both friendly and unfriendly.

The people of the cremation grounds were different. They no longer conceived of themselves as having any social function. Underlying the symbolism of the cremation ground, a kind of possession was taking place of which the highest form was possession by Shiva, or ultimate reality. Surrendering one's body to possession by ultimate reality was, in fact, liberation and the transcendence of one's individual awareness.

What finally emerges from this experience is a state called *mahavyapti*, or "universal integration." This is a state in which all forms of action, perception, knowledge, self, and experience have been unified into intense, total perception, insight, recognition. This form of possession is primitive and powerful. Yet it is also an amazingly sophisticated view of reality that emerges without ever losing contact with a foundational, archaic experience.

These people reached into their core and confronted the brutality of their physical lives. They faced the ephemeral nature of their individuated existence and the terror of life around them. They dealt with the fear and resistance that these things aroused. More than that, they used that fear and resistance as the lever by which they ultimately achieved extraordinary insight.

~

Engaging things that frighten us as pure experience has the potential to take us into a state of profound well-being and an unshakable transcendent awareness. The issue is no longer of purity or impurity or even the acquisition of power. Instead, in what is called "the great banquet," our aim is to consume all forms of experience as nourishment so that we reside in the heart of our hearts.

Having confronted, consumed, and digested everything of which we are afraid, we discover that there is nothing we need fear. We become established within ourselves in a condition of genuine love and respect for all that is Life, seeing all of this as nothing more nor less than our own Self. We have no doubts, no fears, no wants, no needs. There are no issues. There is nothing to analyze and nothing more to know. Our state of surrender is total and profound, and every breath is an act of love.

Through this great banquet, in both its Trika and Krama forms, the Kaula tradition brings that realization down to the level of everyday reality, recognizing that the cremation ground is nothing but the world. The difference is, however, that in the world most people pursue the separate activities of the great banquet without ever understanding the deeper potential implicit within them, wherein lies the real satisfaction. The Kaulas, with their courage and depth of commitment, consumed every limited form of experience and confronted every fear. They lived their everyday lives as nothing but the great banquet, an experience filled with profound joy and well-being in which they observed their deepest selves at work in every manifestation of life.

There is, in this practice, a fusion of immanent and transcendent—a joining of that which is most deeply personal to us and that which is Divine. This creative movement liberates us from every kind of convention and allows us simply to know and be ourselves. It frees us to be in touch with our creative energy and to transcend the limitations of our own mechanism and environment. We realize more and more deeply the infinite potential within us and our capacity to take in every point of view and, instead of becoming scattered and confused, to be nourished and reinforced as we digest everything. In essence, we transcend specific forms of experience to live from the ground out of which all experience springs.

This transcendence of duality is the freedom—the salvation—about which all spiritual systems speak. It is an experience that Dante has characterized as the passing through hell to get to heaven. This is because in a real way the fusion and transcendence of the two is the liberation and recognition of our infinite Self.

In this condition, all experience appears as nothing but the vibrancy of our own being. In fact, it *is* nothing but the vibrancy of our own being. It is similar to the way the sky can be various shades of blue, each one different, each one a part of a spectrum. In the same way, all experience is nothing but variations in a basic resonance that is subtly differentiated due to the interaction with itself. It is from this subtle self-referencing that the whole diverse universe has evolved.

It is not enough to recognize that timeless, spaceless, pure intensity within us, which is also the source of all resonance—of every kind of differentiation, color, texture, tone, and rhythm. We must also go forth in our lives and live that recognition.

Leading a spiritual life is not about pulling away from the world around us to become absorbed within ourselves. It is about first pulling in, intensifying our awareness, and then giving of ourselves. We work to live everyday life with the same openness, clarity, and total surrender that characterizes the Absolute. It resonates in a total openness and a complete, infinite clarity that gives endlessly of itself without ever depreciating its content in any way. This is love and it is what we give ourselves over to.

Through contact with this love, we come to a point where we recognize the highest state within us. This is possible because our minds have become quiet. It is not that we no longer have thoughts, but that the thought process becomes different. Reflecting on my own experience, I find that I don't have thoughts in the way I used to. That is, I can recall a time when thoughts were totally dominant, and another time when thoughts came and went. It is no longer like that. Now there is room to know the Self.

There are a number of mistaken ways to think about the Self. One is to think of it as external to us—as something inaccessible—thus making it a product of our thoughts. Another is to think of it as so different from us that we are unworthy of it. In either case, it is the same mistake—the attempt to seize hold of the Self as we might perceive an object, when actually the Self is always the viewer within us. The Self is a pure internality that encompasses every externality. As we deepen our experience of integration, this becomes more and more apparent.

❧

The most subtle experience of all is the awareness of infinity—living in contact with it continuously even as we observe the functioning of the vital force that manifests in the world as individual experience. Some experiences are wonderful and some are not; each is a mixture of happiness and sadness. But in this context, we never lose contact with the infinity to which we are intimately connected, the infinity which always and forever is. To recognize and dwell in that awareness is the highest stage of spiritual maturity.

Knowing infinity completely rearranges our understanding of time and space. If life is an infinity and if such a thing as eternity exists, then there is no question of getting closer or farther away from it. It simply is, and it is right now. The whole notion of a succession of events evaporates. There is only one thing, and it is our awareness of the infinite presence now pulsating as every experience that is. We feel this in all the different forms and facets that we encounter.

In integration, our ordinary sense of worldly life dissolves. It evaporates in the richness and fullness that we experience pulsating within ourselves. Every moment of every day, we experience our existence as permeated by the love of God. Love rises up within us to be met by love descending. The fusion of the two becomes the recognition of our own nature and of the source of all vitality as one.

Then Life's unlimited aspect flourishes within the context of the boundaries and structures of our individual lives in

time and space without these boundaries coming to domi-
nate us.

⌒

Spiritual development requires careful and intuitive and
continuous observation of the essence of our experiences.
And what is that? It is the pure joy in every moment of joy.
It is the pure anger in every moment of anger. As we
become one-pointed, the straight intensity of each experience slowly unfolds and reveals its own nature. This intensity, recognized in the heart of all experience, takes us into
the state of integration.

INSPIRATION

HERE DOES life in the internal cremation ground take us? Within each person is a need for self-expression. The vitality behind that need reveals itself when we are in a deeply relaxed but alert state. When we are deeply open, that energy expresses itself as inspiration. It simply emerges, manifesting itself in ways that we can learn from.

Early Tantric literature comes under the category of revelation. Even though individual human beings wrote it down, they viewed it not as a personal expression but as something that simply manifested from within them. As they spoke or wrote it, they learned from it themselves. Likewise, when we train ourselves to confront our fears, relax deeply, and open our hearts, a profound understanding emerges from within us that resolves all personal issues. When we are deeply relaxed, an equilibrium extends throughout the whole field of our experience. The inner and the outer merge and we transcend the different anxieties that otherwise permeate our lives. Instead, our lives become an ongoing expression of inspiration.

Every creative effort is a discipline, whether it be music, writing, painting, or anything else. For example, we had better be able to get our fingers on the right piano keys at the right moment or we won't be performing anything very well. There are levels of discipline to any event and every manifestation has a structure. We cultivate this structure in order to be free enough to connect to that inspiration and have it go where it wants to, instead of having our energy run all over the place and get tied up in all kinds of tensions. Just as Arjuna trained intensely to become a warrior, we train ourselves in particular skills. However, we must know when to let go and allow that most vital dimension of our lives to move its way through the skill to express itself as it wills.

In the beginning, the possibility of inspiration having an impact on all levels of our lives is subject to the degree to which our egos are out of the way. Nevertheless, that experience of inspiration can give rise to a kind of vision. For instance, when Arjuna ceased to cling to his fear of particular outcomes, Krishna appeared to him as the whole universe.

Indeed, the rising up of inspiration is a powerful force that changes everything. It changes the understanding we have of ourselves and our potential. Eventually, it articulates itself through our activity and behavior to transform the whole field of our lives.

How does it come about? We practice bringing our attention, with some intensity, concentration, and depth of caring, to the simple process of feeling the flow of vital force within us. Doing this over and over is what matters. It is what allows room for grace to move in, bringing about the coalescing of ever-finer levels of inspiration and ever-deeper opportunities to observe the character of that inspiration itself. And finally, we are established in what we can simply call an inspired state. In this state, it almost appears as though everything we do has an effortless quality of inspiration to it that continuously transforms all it touches.

It boils down to a lot of monotonous work. It is about not

getting caught up in thinking about what hasn't happened for me, what might happen to me, or what is going to happen to me—all of which are permutations of the same thing. Instead, it is about simply doing and doing and doing until we figure it out for ourselves. Someone can explain it to us any number of times. But only our doing it over and over will give us the real understanding of what this experience is and where it leads.

It is just practice—but not just sitting down and practicing meditation. Everything becomes a question of practice as we repeatedly learn to pull ourselves in, to center our attention, and to feel the flow of vital force. We first feel it internally and then externally. This union of internal and external forces is also part of the experience of integration.

In saying this, I am taking two different levels of mundane awareness and practice and suggesting that, by fusing them through our constant attention, we can experience a total transformation in our awareness. However, this happens only through practice.

In my own life, I can honestly say that I am doing one thing, and it is exactly the same practice I was instructed to do the first day I met my teacher Rudi. While it is true that this simple process has expanded in quality and horizon over the years, I am doing nothing significantly different now from what I did then.

Spiritual practice is not about being in our heads. Being in our heads about any of it is simply being in our heads and has nothing useful to offer. Instead of worrying about things, we can choose the alternative—namely, to tune into this creative power within us. We organize ourselves, we deal with whatever tensions present themselves to us, and we don't lie down in front of them. Whatever needs changing, we change. In this way, we create an environment within and around us in which there is a real flow and a depth that allows for a genuine expression of love. If something in our lives obstructs this, my view is that we either get rid of it or open ourselves up to it. In other words, if we look at it and decide that it is not flushable for some reason, then our responsibility is to make it wonderful. This is not anybody else's responsibility.

We can't groan about the lack of love in our lives when we are not giving it every single day ourselves. If our own hearts are not open and putting out love, then how can we expect anybody else's to do so? Be reasonable. If we want love in our lives, we create it. We don't sit and moan because someone isn't coming into our lives and laying on us the love we want. The tooth fairy went out the window when we were six years old.

First, we have to have the depth of commitment, the willingness to work within ourselves, and the capacity to surrender all attachments. Then we have to practice it in every single context. In so doing, we will discover a capacity within us that we never imagined and a transformation in our lives that is wonderful. However, for all the transformation that takes place, the only thing of any value that remains is the depth, the quality, and the richness that we experience within ourselves. And then comes the opportunity to share it with loving people who are also willing to work.

Rudi used to say, "Life is profound only in its simplicity." It is the simple effort we make every day that simplifies us by releasing the tension and crystallization. It is what makes possible a vision of the depth and simplicity of which we are intimately a part and which is also intimately a part of us.

—

Creativity is about taking raw materials and making something greater than the sum of all the individual parts. The highest expressions of creativity in every arena reach into the deepest parts of our spirit and arouse some expansion of that spirit.

—

Sometimes I talk about allowing things to happen; at other times I talk about the need to work. There is actually no contradiction between the two. Padmasambhava, the great

Indian master of the eighth century who first brought Vajrayana Buddhism to Tibet, said, "Even though my vision is as vast as the night-time sky, my behavior is very refined." What he meant by this was that although he was a totally vast person, his behavior was still intentional and disciplined. This was a person who had reached mastery and yet still said, "Be disciplined and concentrated."

In other words, there is something we do have to make happen—and, at the same time, something that we cannot make happen. For example, a master musician makes music happen in a way that transcends the instrument, the musician, and even the music itself. In some sense, we make something happen through our personal effort, discipline, and concentration. We lay the foundation, through practice, for something to happen—we train ourselves to prepare for inspiration. But after that, grace and inspiration do the rest.

Spirituality has everything to do with opening ourselves to that grace and going deeply into that state of inspiration.

~

As we continue to intensify our own inner state, opportunities for creative expression will happen to us. Rudi had a student who is a famous artist and also a fine person. Some years ago, he and I were talking about fame in the world and he said that, basically, you have to concentrate on the quality of your own work and just accept that the energy of that work will attract its own audience, whoever that audience may be.

If we do our own work, the opportunities we require for creative expression will appear. So, we should be greatly concerned with doing good work—and only a little concerned with selling it. Our avenues will appear when we are able to see them. In fact, the truth is that they are there right now. When we let go of our preconceived ideas of how things should turn out, we suddenly see these avenues stretching out clearly before us.

—

Inspiration itself is beyond time and space. It has infinite potential—which doesn't necessarily mean that it manifests infinite potential. That infinite potential will be coaxed forth over time as layer after layer of obstruction, misunderstanding, egotism, and tension are peeled away through our repeated contact with it. Then it is possible that some kind of extraordinary potential may manifest.

—

We experience our real potential when we become still—which takes practice—and feel something subtle build up within us. Most people tend to resist it and get comfortable.

However, if we can just let go and allow it to do its thing, the possibility for bigness starts to happen. Then we can say, "It happened to me. I didn't do it." Although we cultivate ourselves and thereby do something to let this thing happen, we cannot take credit for it. We just have to feel that it has happened.

From the point of view of stillness, there are no wrong choices. There are also no right ones. There are just choices, and we make our lives into what they are. The question then becomes what do we do to facilitate the manifestation of stillness in our lives?

So much of what we struggle for in our lives is illusion. The reality comes when we surrender the illusion and tension, open ourselves to life, and allow that power and infinity to express itself in the field of our creative energy. It is when we cultivate the state of the cremation ground in our own hearts and minds that the potential for bigness enters our lives. But it can't come in when we are busy fussing, fretting, and holding on. We are just disturbing the field and not allowing any greatness of spirit to enter the picture.

⌒

Most people spend their lives trying to prove that what they know is right. Of course, this dooms us to failure because we really know very little. And it is almost worse when we get professional credentials because we are then expected to know something.

This kind of academic or professional knowledge tells us little about the essence of Life Itself. So, on the one hand, we end up deluded about what we think we do know and, on the other, sidetracked from perceiving a deeper knowledge that is available to us every moment of our lives. Our effort, therefore, must be to get in touch with that deeper knowledge.

You might ask, "How do I do that, since *it* is an infinity that I know nothing about?" Well, I'd venture to say that what informs us is the energy itself. All we have to do is quiet our minds, our emotions, and our reactions and stop dwelling on what we think we know. We stop thinking about all that and simply and slowly harmonize ourselves with this inner event. We pay careful attention to each stage that begins to unfold within us in the context of the present moment and deal with each accordingly. This is what allows the situation to inform us.

For example, we can interact with other people and sense everything we need to know about an event without them ever saying a word. We pick up these things by stopping our internal dialogue, by suspending our judgments, and by letting go of our identification with who we think we are and what we think we are doing. Then our own trip becomes

nonexistent and we can begin tuning into the creative energy of the situation itself. When we do that, *it* will give us
access to all of its information and numerous facets. We
can move carefully in harmony with it and promote some
creative end. It is only when we get stuck in some idea about
what that creative end should be that we cause the process
to shut down.

There is a depth within consciousness—which means that
there is a depth within each of us—where there is no longer
any perception. This is a depth that we cannot "think"
about, a depth of such stillness that it is motionless. Thus,
perception or cognizance cannot happen as they usually do.
That domain within us is so beyond any gross vibration
that the capacity for cognizing some "other" disappears.

I bring this up to suggest that we can experience a level of
such profound stillness that, when our awareness is focused
within it, a profound reorganization in our whole system
occurs. From this reorganization, all kinds of change can
flow. This stillness, deep and quiet, is a state in which we
don't recognize ourselves as distinct individuals. We don't
recognize the existence of the outside world or even of any
inner world. There is only a total fusion of the whole.

There is simply no way for us to wrap our minds around
the potential that exists within stillness. We can never know
in advance what is possible or available to us. We cannot

imagine or dream it up, and no matter how intuitive we may be, we cannot possibly grasp the twists and turns of our experiential existence. In fact, it is impossible and even stupid to try. After all, why waste all that energy trying to figure out what's going to happen in the movie when we can sit and quietly watch until it actually reaches the end. Then we know for sure how it all turns out.

What does it mean to live a deeply creative life? If we are really devoted to quality in whatever we do, we will suddenly realize that we can't do everything. The world is like a big dining table serving up lots of different experiences. If we are going to be strong and grow a lot, we have to be thoughtful about which ones we consume and how much energy we spend on them. This is necessary because we have to balance our external creative expression, however we choose to manifest it, with our internal development. We cannot descend and grow at the same time—whether we are talking about business or spiritual growth. Even if our intentions are good, if we intend to "do" anything, one day we are going to wake up and find ourselves out on the end of some limb.

When we are deeply open and our hearts are full, what is there to go and accomplish? What is there to add to the equation? The idea that we should have to go out and fulfill some desire is an immediate indication of exactly what we haven't accomplished. This is because awareness of the highest reality brings a sense of peace and well-being that takes us beyond the notion of want and need, of coming and going.

◦━━

In our inner work, we function as individual filters for the expression of the creative energy. The more refined we become as human beings, the less ambition and activity we manifest in that process. And while it is unlikely that ambition will ever fully cease, as creative people we can engage in something not so much from ambition but rather out of love for what we are doing. By raising whatever we do to the level of an art, we can be concerned with the quality of our understanding and expression and not with the particular form of payback we get.

What we appreciate about art is the skillful articulation of inspiration. We admire a piece of art because it emerges from a subtle feeling that intensifies and condenses into an expression of that power. We likewise admire a person who has the capacity to perform with that same kind of purity and intensity.

Any action at all has the potential for purity, clarity, and intensity when it is a creative expression, a condensation of the vitality of Life Itself articulated in a pure way without a motive or hook in it. Then it simply manifests the power of a person's own soul. To go deeply into that state of inspiration is to recognize that every experience, at its deepest level, is the pure and joyous manifestation of the vitality of our own souls.

⌁

Any inspiration always happens spontaneously, even if we think of it as something that is building toward expression. It happens spontaneously because inspiration itself exists beyond time and space. It is never sequential. Even though there are successive tides in our awareness, at the highest stage everything happens within dynamic stillness; there is no issue of one thing following another. Within an infinity, everything is an infinite vibrancy.

Clarity does not accumulate—it simply flashes forth. The understanding that may accumulate relative to the successful operation of some mechanism, or the effective development of a system fulfilling a certain objective, differs from the experience of clarity. We can accumulate this kind of knowledge, but it is only the basis of a limited understanding of who and what we are as individuals. Even when we accumulate a lot of such knowledge, it is still the source of limitation. Clarity does not accumulate and surrender takes no time.

The dwellers in the cremation ground understood that there is, within us, a level of awareness that permeates both life and death. When we understand this, we find that life and death are really two phases in the articulation of time. There is also a state of consciousness that permeates both of them and transcends time itself.

This is related to the experience of inspiration because the emergence of inspiration within a person is initially an intense flash of insight with no conceptual content to it whatsoever. It is simply a flash that reorganizes our overall system in some way. It is a little bit like getting struck by lightning.

This pure creative power—this pure conscious energy— moves through our systems at various levels, getting structured into a kind of wave that is identified as conceptual content. This translates into some behavioral manifestation—in other words, we enact it. And enacting the idea changes the form of our lives and shows us how inspiration is related to everything.

Can we remember the moment of that first flash of insight—before anything was structured, conceptualized, or enacted? That is the moment in which we experience directly the nature of the highest reality.

I am not exactly a religious person. Still I would have to say that, however we phrase it, it is really God that does everything. We do nothing. In fact, it is hard to accept just how much nothing we really do. Whatever we do in order to try to make things happen is actually more often a matter of stepping on our own feet and creating more problems than solutions. These have nothing to do with our reality but only with our tensions.

In many ways, we all want to feel that we are doing something and that our work has some effect. I am no different. At the same time, it is important that we not take this concern with our impact on the external world too seriously. It is simply not that critical. If something happens, that is fine. If not, that is also fine.

In every kind of effort, a point comes where we mature in it. This doesn't necessarily mean that the endeavor becomes easy, but that the inner discipline we have cultivated supports the manifestation of inspiration. Then it becomes fulfilling. Our attention is no longer focused on the discipline we have established because that pretty much becomes a given. Instead, the discipline allows us to dispense with a lot of the uncertainties in dealing with life so that we can pay attention to what is really important to us.

As a beginner, you do things. As a more practiced person, you don't do anything. You simply observe and experience the vitality of your own essence at work in and around you. This is something like riding the power of a dragon.

⌒

Because we reach again and again to our inner source, a connection is established between our body, mind, and spirit. This connection releases a natural flow of energy. And in a way that becomes clear only through experiencing it, this flow brings about understanding. This flow establishes itself because we surrender our tensions and turn inside again and again. We don't make it happen exactly. It simply happens and only eventually do we recognize it.

We have no control over this process and, paradoxically, this is a great freedom. If we had control over our experience, everything we did would reflect the limits of our imagination and prejudice. Our control would continuously deny us the extraordinary opportunity we have to grow and expand beyond ourselves. It would prevent us ultimately from becoming established in a truth that goes beyond all limitations.

The information we receive about ourselves, about the direction of our lives, about the decisions we must make or refrain from making, about how these decisions should or should not be expressed—all of this comes from inside us. This is possible because we take the time to tune into and cultivate our awareness of our inner Self.

As we observe this vitality functioning within and around us, we begin to appreciate one final and important thing. Even as Krishna shows Arjuna that all individual expressions of life are nothing but Krishna himself, we discover that from the very beginning it has been the creative power of Life Itself functioning from within us and through us in every arena. Slowly, we begin to see that we are on a mysterious and amazing journey in which we have the opportunity for influence but never the possibility for control.

〜

For the person who lives in a state of surrender, everything emerges from within—all imagination and intelligence become present. It is not an issue of becoming one thing or another; it is just a question of being what we are.

This is an endeavor in which pretty much everybody has the right stuff. And appropriate effort will bring unlimited result. The appropriate effort is, first, to master the discipline of our spiritual practice and then, upon that foundation, to live happily. I would also say that in whatever we decide to do in terms of worldly endeavor it is important not to hold back. It is important just to do it and, in the doing, to be happy—no matter what.

In the old television series *Kung Fu*, the blind master would be attacked by opponents, who would try to hit him on the head with staffs or shoot him with arrows. No one had to tell him where the attack was coming from. He always knew and could intercept or dodge the blow. This was not intuition—it was openness. He was so sensitive to his environment that, as each new force entered it, he automatically established balance. And he did so not from his mind, but from a much deeper place.

This is very different from instinct or intuition. It is a natural tendency for our own energy to seek balance and to move toward harmony. This comes from being open. In general, it is best just to be open because in that openness resides a subtle awareness. Our sensitivity to it allows us quickly to see what is happening and to embrace it if such is proper, or to step aside if that is what the situation calls for. From this state, inspiration arises of its own.

At the core of any action is creative energy. That creative power comes together in stillness. A kind of subtle organization forms up within it, which then articulates itself as inspiration.

Consider the moments we feel inspired. Consider the pressures that compel us toward that inspiration. Were we to examine the different moments when a shift occurs and something extends from it, we would find a continuity flowing through each shift, a gradual change of state repeating itself. We would find a steady buildup in which something finally flips and leaves us with a whole different event. This is the fusion of action and inaction—the silent gathering up which combusts in the form of inspiration and is the force by which we go out and act. In this case, action and inaction are really one thing.

Inspired action is whatever we do that brings about a real change in our lives. Starting up a business or getting married or writing a book are actions that can change the pattern of our lives. (Washing the dishes, on the other hand, is just maintenance.) Inspiration sometimes leads us into nonaction. Indeed, sometimes inaction is the most powerful form of action.

～

To surrender the outcome of our actions, to enter the inner cremation ground, to live as the heroes of our own lives— all of these things take us into the inspired life. By cultivating awareness of the profound creativity within us every single day in every single circumstance, we come to a powerful understanding of the nature of the Self and its extraordinary potency, its infiniteness, and our total unity within that. Like Arjuna, we see the Divine face to face. This frees us from every sense of limitation and selfishness, enabling us to serve Life Itself in everything we encounter. Is this not simply serving ourselves?

There is but one soul, and everything around us is an articulation of its pure creative power. To find within ourselves that one soul is to find the same power and joy that have created the whole universe. In that state there is nothing lacking, nothing to be added, and nothing that can ever be taken away.

ABOUT THE AUTHOR

AMERICAN-BORN Swami Chetanananda brings a rich contemporary Western perspective to his articulation of the practice of meditation, spiritual work, and the Eastern philosophy of Kashmir Shaivism. Chetanananda was a close disciple and spiritual teacher under Swami Rudrananda. Initiated into the Indian Saraswati order of monks in 1978 in Ganeshpuri, India, Chetanananda has since established centers throughout the United States, dedicated to the active practice of a spiritual life. In 1981, Chetanananda founded the Nityananda Institute now headquartered in Portland, Oregon. Chetanananda is the author of many works, including *Choose to Be Happy, The Open Moment, The Breath of God, The Logic of Love,* and *Dynamic Stillness Volumes 1 and 2.* Audio recordings include *Meditation: A Guided Practice for Every Day* and *Keys to Mastery.*